BETTER LATE THAN NEVER

TRIGGER™
The mental health & wellbeing publisher

First published in 2020
This edition published in 2023 by Trigger Publishing
An imprint of Shaw Callaghan Ltd

UK Office
The Stanley Building
7 Pancras Square
Kings Cross
London N1C 4AG

US Office
On Point Executive Center, Inc
3030 N Rocky Point Drive W
Suite 150
Tampa, FL 33607
www.triggerhub.org

A CIP catalogue record for this book is available upon request from the British Library
ISBN: 978-1-83796-322-5
Ebook ISBN: 978-1-83796-323-2

Cover design by Bookollective
Typeset by Lapiz Digital Services

ABOUT THE AUTHOR

Emma Mahony is the author of two books published by HarperCollins – *Double Trouble (Twins and How to Survive Them)* and *Stand and Deliver (And Other Brilliant Ways to Give Birth)*. Up until her diagnosis for ADHD, Emma worked as a journalist for *The Times* as Pets, Property, Shopping, Food and Drink, Gardening, and Family Travel editor, and freelanced for the *Financial Times*, the *Guardian*, the *Independent* and the *Telegraph*. Since her diagnosis, she requalified as a secondary school teacher of Spanish and French, and is part of the first cohort of Now Teachers, a charity which supports professionals to make a career change into teaching. She is married with three children and lives between Sussex and London. Furloughed during the pandemic, she set up a podcast — The ADHD Lockdown Diaries — a foodbank scheme delivering over 1500 meals to struggling families in Sussex, and produced the film *Coming Home* for her company Barker January productions.

DISCLAIMER

Trigger encourages diversity and different viewpoints. However, all views, thoughts, and opinions expressed in this book are the author's own and are not necessarily representative of Trigger as an organisation. All material in this book is set out in good faith for general guidance and no liability can be accepted for loss or expense incurred in following the information given. In particular, this book is not intended to replace expert medical or psychiatric advice. It is intended for informational purposes only and for your own personal use and guidance. It is not intended to diagnose, treat or act as a substitute for professional medical advice. The author is not a medical practitioner nor a counsellor, and professional advice should be sought if desired before embarking on any health-related programme.

BETTER LATE THAN NEVER

Understand, Survive and Thrive Midlife ADHD Diagnosis

EMMA MAHONY

TRIGGER™
The mental health & wellbeing publisher

FOR MY FATHER JOHN, WHERE IT ALL STARTED. AND MY SON MICHAEL, WHERE THE TALE CONTINUES.

CONTENTS

THE STORY OF FIDGETY PHILIP

Let me see if Philip can
Be a little gentleman;
Let me see if he is able
To sit still for once at table:
Thus Papa bade Phil behave;
And Mamma looked very grave.
But fidgety Phil,
He won't sit still;
He wriggles,
And giggles,
And then, I declare,
Swings backwards and forwards,
And tilts up his chair,
Just like any rocking-horse –
'Philip! I am getting cross!'
See the naughty, restless child,
Growing still more rude and wild,
Till his chair falls over quite.
Philip screams with all his might,
Catches at the cloth, but then
That makes matters worse again.
Down upon the ground they fall,
Glasses, plates, knives, forks, and all.
How Mamma did fret and frown
When she saw them tumbling down!
And Papa made such a face!
Philip is in sad disgrace.

Excerpt from 'The Story of Fidgety Philip' from the book *Struwwelpeter* by Dr Heinrich Hoffman, published in Germany in 1845. This poem appeared alongside the first published treatise on ADHD in the British medical journal, *The Lancet*, in 1904.

FOREWORD

Better Late Than Never takes the reader on an exciting and informative journey of self-discovery, from understanding the condition to learning to thrive with late-diagnosis ADHD. It is an intimate tour of the inner world of women who have lived with both the struggles and the strengths of undiagnosed, untreated ADHD.

Transparent, honest, and personal, this book goes beyond a mere dry presentation of facts. Emma Mahony beautifully weaves expert facts and contributions into her personal narrative. Through this detailed description of her life and journey with undiagnosed ADHD, from confusion to diagnosis to medication and therapy, we follow Emma as she ultimately comes to know and understand herself.

Having been a therapist for women with ADHD for over thirty years, I can attest to the fact that most women with ADHD symptoms at midlife seem to want to be fixed. Their low sense of self-worth has led them to be isolated from others and alienated from themselves. The small daily assaults to one's sense of self when living with unexplained and untreated ADHD until midlife is untethering and overwhelming.

- They are determined to put off any moves toward a meaningful life until their difficulties are gone.
- They do not feel entitled to pursue personal goals or take power in relationships.
- They have idealized gender-role expectations and have internalized a negative self-view that ignores their positive traits or strengths.

- They are focused almost entirely on what's wrong with them! – They want to run from that part of themselves by hiding, withdrawing, pretending, and retreating.

Women are very often not diagnosed until midlife, as this book clearly explains. Often, they do not have stereotypical symptoms, or these symptoms have been masked by learned compensations, depression, or a high IQ. They grow up without a soothing internalized voice, and with no explanation for their difficulties. Because of this, their core sense of self easily gets "tangled up" with their brain-based differences, and their self-esteem suffers.

These women compare themselves to neurotypical women and often feel like failures as women, wives, mothers, friends and co-workers because their executive-functioning struggles make daily life a battle. Knowing no different, it's natural to assume that everyone is combating the same issues as they are, but doing so more effectively.

Due to all of this, women who are not diagnosed until midlife are in need of healing, of being steered towards acceptance and wholeness, and away from shame and self-blame. This is the goal of counselling for these women, as is discussed in length in this book. It's a subject that's often left out of books on ADHD.

Emma's takeaway message to the reader is critical … The key to living successfully with ADHD as a woman diagnosed at midlife is not to try *get over* who you are or to engage in an exhaustive and defeating battle to *fit in*, but instead to find a *good fit* by channelling your traits.

The true goal for an adult with ADHD (and this is what my life's professional work has centred on) has to be to try and teach people not to keep trying to get over who they are. Rather than hoping to be "fixed", I encourage them to see themselves as whole, with difficulties and strengths . . . as a person with deep values and core traits that define them, ultimately, much more than their ADHD traits do. Emma's journey is the perfect vehicle for this lesson; through her humour and insight, she can continuously widen her horizon by taking in possibilities and options that will bring her greater satisfaction. This is the ultimate lesson in the book – to turn discouragement into hope and give the reader the belief in the *possibility* of moving from surviving to thriving, despite their diagnosis. Getting to the point where one can start to believe this is possible, is the first and most important step in a journey to wholeness and healing.

Emma Mahony is a great ADHD role model, demonstrating through her courage to persist despite her struggles that with the right support we can use our natural desire to innovate and create, to make meaningful contributions and lead fulfilling lives.

***

Sari Solden's *Women with Attention Deficit Disorder* was written in 1995, updated in 2005, and has often been described as a book that "saved my life". Female readers claim to recognise themselves within it and no longer feel alone, after a lifetime of secretly hiding their challenges. Her second book *Journeys through ADDulthood* (Walker & Company) first published in 2002 and was released in 2020 as an audiobook. Solden has spoken at over 100 national and international conferences, as well as maintaining a private practice in Ann Arbor, Michigan in the US.

Her latest publication, a self-help workbook called *A Radical Guide for Women with ADHD: Embrace Neurodiversity, Live Boldly and Break Through Barriers* was co-authored with Dr Michelle Frank and tells the stories of women who have shown up in their practices over the years, and aims to overcome negative self-talk, discover strengths, build meaningful relationships, and resist cultural stigma.

sarisolden.com

By Sari Solden, MS, Therapist, Speaker and Author of *Women with Attention Deficit Disorder*

TEN THINGS TO KNOW ABOUT ADHD

1) It was first described as "minimal brain dysfunction", then "hyperkinetic disorder"; in 2004 it became ADD (Attention Deficit Disorder), and now is generally termed ADHD (Attention Deficit Hyperactivity Disorder).
2) Its three traits are impulsivity, restlessness, and distractibility.
3) Many successful entrepreneurs, comedians, actors, sportsmen, artists, and musicians have ADHD, including entrepreneur Richard Branson, comedian Rory Bremner, actors Johnny Depp, Channing Tatum and Emma Watson, Olympian Michael Phelps, racing driver Lewis Hamilton, and musician Will.i.am.
4) It is a neurodevelopmental disorder[1], *not* a behavioural one. This rules out the theory that it is down to poor parenting, too much TV, junk food, and other myths.
5) It is similar in heritability to height. Around 80% of cases are inherited from one or both parents.
6) It affects 3–8% of the population, regardless of gender or race. However, boys are three times more likely to be diagnosed than girls. 90% of children or teens with it experience classroom behavioural or emotional problems, peer relationship problems in school, low academic attainment, school suspensions, or expulsions[2].
7) If left undiagnosed and untreated, it can develop into the more serious Oppositional Defiant Disorder (ODD) or conduct disorder.

---

1 Williams, N.M., et al., *'Rare chromosomal deletions and duplications in attention-deficit hyperactivity disorder: a genome-wide analysis'* *The Lancet*. Volume 376, issue 9750 (2010) pp. 1401–1408.

2 Barkley, R.A., *Managing ADHD in Schools* (Eau Claire WI: PESI inc 2016).

8) People with ADHD have lower levels of the brain chemical dopamine, which regulates movement and attention, and is linked to addiction. ADHD does not affect intelligence.
9) Around 20% of the prison population suffers from undiagnosed ADHD, according to a study by the UK Adult ADHD network.
10) Unlike other neurodevelopmental conditions, such as autism, ADHD can be safely treated with medication (and diet, exercise, and lifestyle changes).

PREFACE

DIARY ENTRY: 17 JANUARY, 2016

Yesterday I was diagnosed with ADHD. It was a long time coming – fifty-one years, to be precise – and the diagnosis was remarkably swift when it came. The process was painful, as painful as sitting in the dentist's chair, and the information that the psychiatrist needed to extract was not sugar-coated, or balanced with the positives; it was bald and barefaced – and the responses had to be black and white. It was a long interview, an hour and a half, but that's not long to sum up a life – especially if you are going to change that life with a diagnosis at the end of it.

Dr Jain had pages and pages of questions to ask, and he wanted me to be very precise with my answers. The answers I could use were "often, very often, seldom, or not all", but sometimes the questions didn't quite fit. And yet, if he seemed robotic in his quick-fire approach, and batted away any attempts from me to pin him down on the meaning of the words, he never seemed to be reading from a script. It was like the questions were a knife to pierce through my carapace of half a century, to get to me before I had time to think of or sculpt answers. He wanted the questions answered impulsively, intuitively, before I could reflect. Either that or he was in a tearing hurry to get on to the next person.

The result of that day and that diagnosis is this book.

INTRODUCTION

"Fall down seven times, stand up eight."
Japanese Proverb

This book is about late diagnosis of ADHD in an adult (anyone over 18), but more specifically about late diagnosis of ADHD in women, an area that has been much less researched and somewhat overlooked. This complex issue tackles mental health, and is written for anyone who has ever struggled with their brain, and felt shame at being unable to function like others, or who may see clearly that a loved one has all the traits of ADHD, and wants to know what to do. If you are picking this book up as a medical practitioner, hungry for a deeper personal understanding of how ADHD can affect patients, particularly female ones, you will find plenty of honest accounts of the mash-ups within my life and truth in the detail of how the traits have affected it. My personal story, interwoven with all the science and references to medical studies, focuses only where the ADHD has shown up in my life, so may seem a little heavy on the disaster stories at times.

MY STORY

Because of the way my brain is wired, I can't help but get things wrong. Even at the age of one, when I learnt to speak, I would say everything backwards[3]. Butter was 'tubba', birds were 'dubbies', and it took a while for my parents to transpose the letters and see that I was making sense.

---

3 Camarata, S. M. and Gibson, T, Pragmatic Language deficits in ADHD. *MRDD research reviews*, 5, (1999) pp. 207–214.

The merest trifles that most people do naturally – arriving to places on time, remembering their wallet, not losing things such as keys, mobile phones, and credit cards constantly, paying fines, avoiding speeding tickets, etc. – are rather boring things at which to excel in my world. I've made them that way so as not to beat myself up when I fail at them regularly. However, the older I get, the more I realise that these boring things are actually important, and how exasperating it is for people when they think that I do them 'on purpose' or, more recently since my diagnosis, that I 'use ADHD as an excuse'. ADHD is not a moral failing; it is a neurological one. It is not 'all in your head', and there's no 'subconscious intention to forget something' – as one therapist continually suggested before diagnosis. It is just that I am neuroatypical.

One of my earliest school memories is of combing the grass around my walk to school in search of an exercise book that held all my homework. I'd lost it somewhere, somehow, and I was genuinely scared as I traced and retraced the steps along my daily journey. I knew that my headmistress might beat me with a horse-riding crop across the back of my legs for losing it, because I'd been beaten before by her, for seemingly smaller "trifles" such as mucking around in the lunch queue, bored.

I was seven years old.

What I didn't know then is that not even her beatings would stop me from losing things. I've never been able to "learn" that particular lesson. Only yesterday, forty-five years later, I was retracing my steps along a six-mile dog walk, this time trying to find a credit card that had dropped out of my pocket. I lose things constantly, and was practising "non-attachment" to things before I could even spell "Buddhism".

As a young girl, I was a tomboy. From around the age of seven, I refused to leave the house if my mother made me wear a skirt, and I was more likely to be roller-skating, or riding down the road with my arms folded on my bicycle, than playing with dolls. Being a tomboy gave me an excuse to engage in more physical and risky activities, such as climbing trees and jumping off rocks into rivers. I had two brothers, and quickly learnt that girls seemed to have a really boring hand dealt to them in the days of "Barbie Does the Ironing".

It appears my experience was more typical than I knew. Psychotherapist and author of *Women with Attention Deficit Disorder*, Sari Solden comments: 'The problem for women is that most of them were not diagnosed as children. Even if they were hyperactive, they usually did not act out in the same way boys did. They were apt to be labelled tomboys or written off in some other way without understanding the underlying attention deficit disorder.'

Like some people, you may wonder if ADHD is actually "real". A few years ago, a book called *ADHD Does Not Exist*[4] was published to great critical acclaim. The author, a behavioural neurologist, argued that ADHD described a cluster of symptoms that were also present in twenty other conditions from bipolar to giftedness and depression – and didn't exist as a separate disorder. The timing of this book chimed with fears of an ADHD "epidemic" in the media, and a statistical rise in offering young children medication, with anxiety around medicalising childhood and playing into the hands of "big pharma". Many of the traits were put down to bad parenting, like the time when my father suggested that what my ADHD son Michael really needed was "a jolly good thumping", and who can't point the finger at any mother or father and find them wanting?

So when I hear of today's fears around a rising diagnosis of ADHD in children or adults – usually tapping into worries around taking medication – my response is different than most. I feel thankful: rising diagnoses means that this invisible condition is at last being brought into the light. And with that recognition, will (hopefully) come understanding and compassion. Because, to quote from the Eeyore of experts on the condition, the author of more than nineteen books on

---

4 Saul, R, *ADHD Does Not Exist: The Truth About Attention Deficit Hyperactivity Disorder*. (New York: Harper Wave, 2014).

the subject, Dr Russell Barkley: *This is a very serious disorder … As adults, people with ADHD are five times more likely to speed and three times more likely to have their licences revoked than other people. They're more likely to experience accidental injuries – burns, poisoning, traffic accidents, and all kinds of trauma – than other people. In fact, having ADHD makes you three times more likely to be dead by the age of forty-five.*[5]

Yikes. I'm bloody lucky to be alive.

So, in the following pages, I'll expose why I believe it's a condition whose time has come; why I am thankful that the approach to disciplining children has changed dramatically in a single generation, so that my son, who was first diagnosed with ADHD aged twelve in the last year of primary school, won't have to suffer the indignity of being put over someone's lap and caned as his mother was. This was the headmistress's last resort in our small private school, despite her being fond of me. And believe it or not, I also used to argue in favour of corporal punishment in school debating lessons, because it was over and done with quickly, and I preferred that approach to the hours I spent facing the wall outside of the classroom, counting the bumps on the wallpaper. It was so boring being excluded from the class.

When asked at the 2014 International Conference on ADHD what the overriding sense of having the condition is like, the motivational speaker and author of *Movers, Dreamers and Risk-Takers*, Kevin Roberts, said: 'It is like having a giant foam finger pointing at my forehead saying, "You Are Wrong!"'

It is true. Few children with ADHD will emerge from school without a battering to their confidence. I learnt about being ashamed of my shortcomings from an early age, and quickly invented ways of covering them up. I used to memorise joke books because I saw how quickly humour could diffuse a situation. Charm, complimenting teachers on their dress sense sometimes worked, as did effusive politeness in the face of being caught or found out. And yet underneath this bluff lurked a sense of shame – and

---

5 Foley, D, *Growing up with ADHD* <http://time.com/growing-up-with-adhd/> [accessed 1 August 2018].

shame is a dangerous emotion. It carries with it the whiff of something unclean, not quite right; something to hide, not to show others – and still does today. Shame is a lonely feeling; it is suffused with a sense of unworthiness of love, of somehow not fitting in or being good enough.

Recently, I went to a memorial service of a university friend who struggled with his mental health all of his life, despite holding down an impressive job in the city. That he decided to take his own life without telling a soul – making plans with friends and family just the day before, and with a full contacts book and calendar – spoke to me about the power of shame. Rather than reveal the extent of his loneliness or struggles, he chose to overdose on his medication. A church service packed with his friends, colleagues, and family, who'd given up their work time to be there on a Monday afternoon, showed just how easily he could have reached out instead.

Shame can be a killer. And shame's little sister, anxiety, also needs watching. It is impossible to lose or forget things, or let others down constantly, without being affected. Underneath the humour and charm that I worked at so hard to cover up the deficiencies, there was a puzzling lack of trust in myself that could manifest as a lack of confidence at unexpected moments. It didn't seem to fit with my outgoing, extroverted personality. The ADHD might have been masked by a chutzpah and an expensive education, but I lived in constant fear of being exposed in some way or other. I was a personality riddle to others and myself, seemingly bright yet always "letting myself down".

It is also a miracle that I haven't had more brushes with the law, given the statistics around this disorder. Perhaps it was deliberate that I was attracted to a criminal barrister for my husband. If all else failed, I knew he might be useful in court. Now, still married after twenty-five years, and with three adult children of our own, I tell him to get his own dinner party disaster stories and stop telling mine.

Like many ADHD diagnoses that come in middle age, commonly out of their child's diagnosis, mine was the beginning of an understanding into why I'd often caused mayhem around me (and usually walked away pointing the finger at others). As a journalist who had worked on national newspapers here in the UK, the more I looked into this complex condition with my research hat on, the more I understood why I was so well suited to my job of deadlines and an ever-changing roster of stories to work on. I also understood why I was attracted to certain friends, some of whom have had complicated and difficult lives (although only two have a formal diagnosis, both after a long struggle with a misdiagnosis for bipolar disorder and medication that didn't work).

You can imagine how annoying the three traits of ADHD – impulsivity, restlessness and distractibility – are at an early age. My parents tell me they had complaints from the neighbours in the flat below when I was still a baby in my cot, because I used to fidget and make the cot squeak.

A DIFFERENCE, NOT A DEFICIT

For all the under-achievement, knocked self-esteem, and cost to society that accompanies this disorder (remember the statistic that an estimated 20% of prisoners have undiagnosed ADHD[6]), there is also a positive cage-rattling quality and creativity that comes with being wired differently.

You see, for my son, and for me, to have ADHD is not lesser, it isn't even a serious impairment – it just *is*. And I am hopeful that the leaps that have happened towards acceptance of gay marriage in the Western world, and curing HIV and AIDS (once called the "gay plague") will also happen in my son's generation towards understanding and accepting neurodiversity. Soon people with ADHD might be open about it at a job interview (something advised against on every online forum) – like I did at mine when I decided to retrain as a secondary school teacher after my

6 Hill, A, All prisoners to be tested for ADHD, 2009, <https://www.theguardian.com/uk/2009/dec/27/adhd-prisons-mental-health-crime> [accessed 1 August 2018].

diagnosis. Soon after, I performed my own show on ADHD at the Edinburgh Fringe Festival, because I felt driven to overcome the stigma, raise awareness, and open up the conversation around it. There is so much that can be done once you get a diagnosis, to help you live well and understand the condition, that I wanted to be involved in educating others around it, too.

The theme of the 2016 ADHD Awareness Month in the US was "knowing is better". While tabloid newspapers continue to rail against the rising number of diagnoses, I firmly believe that knowledge is power. Diagnosis is a double-edged sword in middle age; it brings with it grief and regret for what might have been, but, ultimately, it offers a responsibility to use the gifts and time we have left to be the change in the world that we want to see, to paraphrase Gandhi. There are so many pros to processing the world differently, there is no need to concentrate on the cons.

THRIVING, NOT STRIVING

Nobody can emerge from a positive diagnosis as quite the same person. This book will show you the benefits of accepting ADHD in your life, how it will help you in multiple ways, from finding the courage to seek accommodations in your workplace, to parenting better, to having better relationships with your partner or friends, to knowing how to take care of yourself in a healthy way when the inevitable overwhelm descends. But I don't want to think of ADHD as something you have to endure, because I believe deep down that ADHDers have more to contribute to the world than some box-ticking neurotypicals would have us believe. We thrive in situations that others abhor, such as crises; we think outside of the box; we have an energy if our interest is piqued that means that we go the extra mile to find an answer or discover a cure.

I wouldn't be surprised if the coronavirus vaccine is discovered by someone who comes out later as an ADHDer, pulling his or her second all-nighter in the laboratory when all others have gone home exhausted. In a state of hyperfocus, we can smash

Olympic records (see page 91), and the fact that award-winning racing drivers, artists, musicians, actors, comedians, inventors, and scientists have this brain proves that it can sometimes be a brilliant, not a bad, thing.

But first, you have to realise that diversity doesn't only apply to race or gender, and that neurodiversity is equally worthy of positive attention to overcome the shame that surrounds any whiff of mental health difference. Ultimately, this book is about hope, about someone who never really understood herself very well until she had a diagnosis, and then found that it was a liberation from a lifetime of covering up and blaming others for her misfortunes. Now, I leap into situations others would spend a lifetime avoiding, simply because I know how I work. I welcome the chaos sometimes, because I am comfortable with it, just as I equally crave structure and order.

HOW TO USE THIS BOOK

The book is divided into three parts:

- **Part 1** helps you understand this highly complex neurodevelopmental disorder.
- **Part 2** explains how to survive with it in a neurotypical world.
- **Part 3** helps you thrive with the knowledge that you are wired differently brain-wise.

I hope you, the reader, find the answers you are looking for in the following pages, or, at the very least, are entertained by my account of a life blundering around in the dark until I found the light switch. This is a serious condition, but my approach is somewhat lighthearted. I can't help it. The one thing that has been my biggest saviour has always been humour. So forgive me if I trip lightly over some of the heavier aspects sometimes.

TEN OF THE MOST COMMON THINGS LOST IN THE UK ANNUALLY

I have always wondered about the disproportionate amount of time I spend looking for my glasses in order to find the other thing I have lost, and how that adds up over the years. Recently, Privilege insurance[7] carried out a survey of how long people in the UK spent looking for things they have lost, and found that people spend six and a half days of their life searching just for the remote control for the TV. This led me to wonder what the figure might be for someone with ADHD. Here are the top ten most commonly misplaced items in the UK.

1) Remote controls
2) Glasses
3) Keys
4) Mobile phone chargers
5) Socks and underwear
6) Pens
7) Wallets/purses
8) Headphones
9) Shoes
10) Bank cards

[7] *I-newspaper*, 24 January, 2020, p.2.

PART 1

UNDERSTANDING ADHD

CHAPTER 1
WHAT ADHD IS – AND IS NOT

"Knowing is Better"
Slogan for ADHD Awareness Week, 2016

So, what is Attention Deficit Hyperactivity Disorder or ADHD? Firstly, it's a misnomer, a poorly phrased description, a seemingly catch-all acronym that inaccurately describes an inability to *regulate* emotion, interest, and attention as a *deficit*. It's described as a "Hyperactivity Disorder", even though one of the three presentations includes a form that is "inattentive" only. Before 1987, it was known as Attention Deficit Disorder and the "inattentive" form is still sometimes referred to as that. However, with or without the hyperactivity, Attention Deficit Hyperactivity Disorder is the current description we are stuck with, so I'll use it for the purposes of this book.

When describing what it is – and how the three traits of restlessness, distractibility, and impulsivity play out, particularly in an adult's life – it is helpful to understand what ADHD is *not*.

PSEUDO-ADHD

Most people think that everyone is a bit ADHD, that our culture is increasingly making us that way as pre-verbal children and pre-care-home adults spend much of their waking time looking at big and small screens, rushing around, being busy.

If aliens landed on planet Earth tomorrow and hung around on our public transport system to see how our society functioned, they'd see millions of earthlings jabbing their fingers at their smartphones, or their faces illuminated like miniature blue moons in front of their laptops, barely noticing their green-headed neighbour (unless they had ADHD and spotted them on the far platform).

My family is no different to the rest of the nation. A typical scene might be my ADHD son playing Xbox ('Turn that sound down!') against some other teenager in Japan, while my elder son watches a movie on his smartphone (how can he bear the teensy size of the screen?) with earphones in, my daughter uploading photos on to Instagram, my husband answering work emails on his phone, while I try to get their attention to sit at the table for dinner. This scene is what psychiatrist and ADHD specialist Dr Ned Hallowell calls "pseudo-ADD" because despite the fact that it might look like scattered attention, mind-wandering, and a lack of concentration, it is nothing to do with ADHD.

So pseudo-ADHD is all around us and deemed acceptable in our Western culture, from the mobile phone that interrupts and demands answering when we are having an intimate dinner with an old friend, to the expectation of school children to have their phones on them at all times, vibrating in their pockets.

"We are all ADHD now!" comes the rallying cry from the *Daily Mail* leader writers. The ADHD tidal wave with its increasing diagnoses year on year is just an excuse for bad parenting, or laziness and lack of discipline in kids, isn't it? While many people may be temporarily silenced by the fascination of what is on their mobile, when the charge finally drains out and they are forced to find something else to do – drift off to read a book, fix that broken fence, attend to bills or mow the lawn – that's when the ADHD becomes evident. What the ADHD person will be left with is a restlessness, the butterfly brain that finds it harder than the rest to settle down to that homework that needs doing (ADHD child) or that tax return that is two years overdue (ADHD adult) and will allow, instead, a mounting anxiety to begin to gnaw away in the pit of the stomach, often closely followed by a negative internal chatter of 'Why can't I get my act together?"/What's wrong with me?'/'Why does everyone else seem to manage?' Eventually such negative self-talk either motivates adults with ADHD into action, because they can't bear it any longer, or they carry on procrastinating in front of a card game on their computer, or distract themselves with self-medication – alcohol or marijuana (to relax), more caffeine (a stimulant to help focus) or cigarettes, sex, videogaming, porn, running; anything that will take the edge off the constant mental restlessness and sometimes physical restlessness that accompanies this condition, and has done all their life.

And that is the point. Someone who is neuroatypical and has ADHD has not developed pseudo-ADHD as a result of living in our caffeine-fuelled, restless, twenty-four hour, always-on-call, high-octane Western culture, or because he or she has just purchased the latest iPhone. This has *always* been their way of operating.

GO FIGURE

The estimated 7% of children and 3% of adults[8] who have ADHD may reach their thirties, forties, fifties, or even sixties and think: 'How come I am the only person at the dinner table, pouring another glass of wine when everyone else wants to go to bed?' or 'How come I am the only person I know who brings a wrap of cocaine/marijuana joint to parties when everyone else seems to have grown out of that habit?' 'What's wrong with everybody?' the ADHDer might ask.

I was surprised to learn early on in my diagnosis that adults with ADHD have "poor self-regard", so we may have a tendency to think the world is wrong – and only we are right. A sort of me-against-the-world tendency, which is also a curious form of self-preservation, that keeps the ADHDer battling on regardless, despite the odds, swimming against the current, thinking it is everyone else and not them.

---

8 CHADD, *General Prevalence of ADHD*: <https://chadd.org/about-adhd/general-prevalence/> [accessed 12 August 2018].

IS IT ME, OR IS IT ADHD?

I have a theory that people will always justify the way they behave, however badly it might seem to others. So even convicts in jail, a number of whom I've interviewed for newspaper articles, will have made sense of their crimes in their head. If you have ever spoken to the two sides of a divorced couple, they each have perfectly valid reasons for why their marriage failed – and usually it has nothing to do with their own failings, and everything to do with their partner's. People make up stories to make sense of their lives, and usually their versions are sweeter than the real truth.

I mention this because, at this stage of the book, you might be thinking: What has this woman got that I haven't got? Isn't ADHD just a giant excuse for the things I struggle with? We all have difficulties keeping our kids on track at school, doing the boring but necessary jobs in life, reducing the washing pile to less than "a mountain" (as one Spanish au pair called it), looking after our wallets/keys/bags. The difference is we don't write a book about it, or talk about complicated acronyms as a disorder. We so-called "normal" people just *deal* with it. This is most people's take and it is the problem that ADHDers, especially women, come up against, despite the condition being around for a hundred years, backed by hundreds of thousands of medical studies[9] and big pharma companies inventing expensive medication to reduce its effects.

And the mountain of washing is just the start of it, because as psychotherapist Sari Solden says in her book *Women with Attention Deficit Disorder*, what happens to a woman with ADHD is that a disproportionate amount of her time is spent finding things that she just put down *somewhere*, and now has lost. Corralling the piles of disorder around the house is a mountain in itself, to be climbed daily. Add to that a sense of time that doesn't seem to chime with others, what clinical psychologist Russell Barkley describes as a "blindness to past, future and time more generally, as well as an

---

[9] More than 34,000 references to ADHD in studies on the US National Library of Medicine [online] [accessed 3 August 2018] Available from https://www.ncbi.nlm.nih.gov/

inability to direct behaviour toward the future and sustain it"[10], and suddenly you have a recipe for a day that can unravel quickly. Of course, there are ways around this (e.g. keys with giant key chains have to go into the key bowl *immediately*), but remember, most adults with ADHD are undiagnosed, so attempt to operate like everyone else (and beat themselves up when they can't). Like physically disabled people who want to use the normal changing rooms at the swimming pool to avoid the stigma, people with ADHD believe they should be able to keep hold of their bag like everyone else, so shouldn't need a special routine or giant yellow tote to do so.

With this thinking, sometimes the house can become a sort of prison. A prison that I avoid by sitting in my car and putting off the moment when I have to go in and face the overwhelming avalanche of boring tasks that present themselves on my way up to my study. I think of the artist Louise Bourgeois's sculpture *Femme Maison* (literally "house wife"), where the woman is pinned down with a house covering her face. It's hard to leave when there are so many unfinished tasks to do (and you've lost your keys again anyway). Would it surprise you to learn that we have never locked our house in the countryside in ten years, unless going on holiday, because it is easier than getting new keys cut regularly, or being locked out?

Sari Solden describes this overwhelm as the key feature of adult female ADHD: a woman who spends so long on routine tasks that she often doesn't have time for the work or creative outlets that sustain her. Solden places disorganisation as the key feature that pushes the ADHD adult to the brink.

As subsequent chapters will show, addiction or depression, for example, can often be what therapists call a "presenting symptom". It might be the reason you seek help for something, only to learn down the line that perhaps ADHD is the underlying itch that is causing the scratchiness.

---

10 Barkley, R.A., Attention-deficit/hyperactivity disorder, self-regulation, and time: towards a more comprehensive theory. *Journal of Developmental and Behavioral Pediatrics* vol. 18(4) (1997), pp. 271–9.

So the pseudo-ADHD that is all around us is not helping the confusion around understanding exactly what this complex disorder is. While it provides a good mask for the ADHDer to allow them to fit right in with others, it is something totally different to having the neurodevelopmental difference all your life.

One of the first things a good ADHD psychiatrist will do is to screen out reasons why the patient may feel they have it, whether that's a recent bereavement, divorce, drug addiction or depression (or the purchase of a new Xbox).

WHAT'S IN A NICKNAME?

What's in a nickname? A lot. Nicknames, the cruel childhood tags given to you by family, friends, or even enemies, can be a curiously useful starting point when weeding out pseudo-ADHD from the real thing. Did you ever have one?

For example, my son who has ADHD was called "The Mikey Barker Show" by his twin's godmother, who used to marvel at his ability to stand on tables, smash plates, and generally do all the things that he was not really supposed to be doing.

Mine, given to me by my father – was "Scatter Brain", or earlier still – "Fidgety Phil" (see page 1). "Fidgets" was another early name for ADHDers. So, if such things were known back in the day, and we'd had the power of Facebook – whose Adult ADHD page is called Phil Fidgety – my route to diagnosis might have been quicker.

The Fidgety Phil tag suggests that I had the hyperactive presentation. To get to sleep at night up to the age of around ten, I would either sit up in my bed and rock, or bang my head against the pillow until eventually I went to sleep. This isn't necessarily a trait – at my ADHD diagnosis, the psychiatrist looked at the nurse and said, 'That's a new one,' but it shows how far a child with ADHD might need to go to calm the restlessness.

A woman I met at the ADHD International Conference told me her name was Jennifer Wood, and her nickname was "Jennifer Would, Wouldn't She", hopefully referring to her impulsivity. Similarly, an ADHD girlfriend of mine, recently diagnosed in her early fifties and also a journalist, had a nickname of "Butterfly

Brain". Jennifer Lawrence, the Hollywood actress, has talked about being a hyperactive child, who took medication for social anxiety. Her nickname was "Nitro", as in "Nitroglycerine".[11]

So, as we've established, it's likely that yours or your loved one's ADHD – if it is genetic – has been around from the very beginning. So, if you are reading this for yourself, what did your family call you?

PROFILE OF A COMPLEX ADHD ASSESSMENT

To show just how complex it can be to find the ADHD there among the many other presenting symptoms or comorbidities that can build up or be present in an adult, have a look at this composite case, written by psychiatrist Judith Mohring, who diagnoses ADHD in patients.

Jane was referred to me by her GP for an ADHD assessment as she was having difficulty concentrating at work and was noticeably hyperactive. On assessment she described low mood, severe anxiety, low self-esteem, and intrusive nightmares and flashbacks to an abusive relationship. The initial diagnosis was one of moderate depression and post-traumatic stress disorder (PTSD). She received treatment with an SSRI antidepressant, sleep advice, and therapy including eye movement desensitisation (EMDR), and psychoeducation. She had a good response. After six months her depression had lifted and her PTSD was much easier to manage. However, the problems with concentration were still there, so an assessment was made for ADHD. This confirmed the diagnosis and treatment with stimulants was started. Her symptoms and functioning improved further and she was able to get a promotion at work and start a new relationship.

11 Levy, M, *Jennifer Lawrence, la muse de Hollywood*, 2013 <http://madame.lefigaro.fr/celebrites/jennifer-lawrence-muse-de-hollywood-151113-630012> [accessed August 2018].

CHAPTER 2
THE TRAITS

"If the practitioner knows his own mind clearly, he will obtain results with little effort. But if he does not know anything about his own mind, all of his effort will be wasted."

Zen Buddhist Master Thuong Chieu

So, I've given some sense of what ADHD is not, so what exactly is it? ADHD consists of three traits: restlessness, impulsivity, and distractibility. However, when psychiatrists diagnose it, they categorise it under three "presentations" (formerly "subtypes"), which are inattentive, hyperactive, or mixed (both hyperactive and inattentive). Which presentation fits which person is worked out on a scoring chart of nine traits, and if you score anything over five out of nine as an adult, you qualify for a particular presentation (it's six or above for children). Currently these traits need to have been present for six months only, but often psychiatrists may also be looking for evidence that it has been there since the early years.

Both my son Michael and myself were diagnosed as "primarily inattentive" (that's basically ADHD without the hyperactive). Michael scored eight out of nine for inattentive presentation (and only five out of nine for hyperactive). My diagnosis in the UK was on the National Health Service, so didn't give the scores. As my NHS psychiatrist pronounced "you either have it or you don't". Michael's diagnosis was done privately, on a company health insurance plan (which is now no longer available with AXA-PPP

Healthcare, interestingly enough). In the States, which is a good ten years ahead of the UK in its understanding and treatment, ADHD is graded as mild, moderate or severe as a spectrum disorder, usually using the *Diagnostic and Statistical Manual*, edition five (DSM-5). As well as the more common genetic type, the neurodevelopmental disorder can be attributed to a traumatic brain injury or prematurity.

DSM-4 VS DSM-5

The sub-heading above may look like a gladiator's battle, but it does in fact refer to the real diagnostic criteria (the old and new versions) that any trained doctor will use to diagnose ADHD. A lot of fuss has been made about the new diagnostic criteria since "the Bible" – DSM-5 – came out in May 2013. Up until then, everyone used the "Old Testament" – DSM-4 – which required the child or adult to have "impairment", a fancy word for being messed up good and proper. Today's "New Testament" says the symptoms only need to be "present" in more than two settings – i.e. home or school (child) or home and work (adult). Therefore the criteria have become less critical, because there is no longer a need to prove to the doctor that yours or your child's life is in obvious trouble because of the symptoms, before getting a diagnosis.

Another change between yesterday's book and today's bible is that instead of requiring these symptoms to have been present from the age of six, today they can have been present from the age of twelve.

Finally, the new DSM-5 makes a greater nod towards adult ADHD than DSM-4, describing what the symptoms might look like in the workplace, for example, and accepting that you may qualify for adult ADHD with only five out of a possible nine symptoms instead of six. One other noteworthy point is that the three *presentations* of ADHD are no longer called "types". Dr David Rabiner, who gives a good, lengthy explanation on the Attention Deficit Disorder Association (ADDA) website[12] suggests that this is to reaffirm the idea that ADHD has a fluidity, that symptoms can

---

12 See Link here: www.add.org/?page=DiagnosticCriteria

change or improve with age, and that the symptoms you show up with today may have transformed into something else by the next time you check in.

GIRLS VS BOYS

ADHD can also show up differently in girls and boys, and it is girls who are often overlooked – the condition is three times more likely to be undetected in girls compared to boys. While an inattentive girl might dreamily look out of the classroom window or, if she has hyperactive ADHD, be over-talkative, a boy is more likely to act out physically. For this reason, ADHD psychiatrist Dr Ned Hallowell says that the biggest indicator for ADHD in girls at school is when they underachieve for their intelligence. However, girls may compensate by working harder, or asking for tutors, or finding some study tricks to keep up, so again diagnosis may not be sought until later in life.

Girls may not even get into trouble at school, although Hallowell's view is that if they are underachieving, ADHD may likely be the cause. In fact, if you need proof, it will be right there in the school reports. In my reports there were phrases, such as "lack of organisation", "mind-wandering", "absentmindedness", "scatter-brained", and even though today more encouraging terms are used, such as "lack of focus", the reference to an inability to concentrate will be there somewhere in the teacher's predictions.

I don't know if I go along with psychiatrist Dr Daniel Amen's somewhat dated view that: "The cultural stereotypes that we have of little girls contribute to their under-identification … as the school system tolerates underachievement in girls that it wouldn't in boys."[13] But I would say that girls often have the social skills to cover it up.

Sari Solden says, "I feel that these girls usually fall into the 'nice little girl' stereotype. Because they are nice, quiet or shy, they meet cultural expectations, so people either don't notice or are not as concerned with their subtle information-processing problems." And

---

13 Solden, S, *Women with Attention Deficit Disorder* (Nevada City: Underwood Books, 2005), p. 57.

just to make things even more complex to spot, primarily inattentive ADHD does not always manifest as lack of attention in class, either. If there is a subject that the girl loves or is really interested in, she may simply put in a lot more extra effort and therefore do well. As my Latin teacher Mr Parsons commented in my school reports used for my diagnosis, the issue could be "learning to concentrate when the matter did not catch her fancy". Without playing into the hands that enforce cultural stereotypes, girls with ADHD often have fewer learning problems with maths and reading in the earlier grades than boys, which, according to Dr Hallowell[14], is another reason that they may not be spotted at school.

UNDERSTANDING HYPERFOCUS

Hyperfocus (HF) is similar to the psychological term "flow", when you are engaged in an activity you enjoy and lose track of time, except it is particular to ADHD (and not always positive). It is a relatively new area of understanding of ADHD and hasn't been researched much, although everyone with ADHD is probably able to point to a period when they experienced it. Currently not included in the DSM-5 criteria (see page 37), perhaps because it is the very opposite of how ADHD is described. It is a complex aspect of ADHD to explain, particularly to non-believers, due to the mismatch between the three traits of ADHD – restlessness, impulsivity, and distractibility – and the ability to spend hours in front of the television, or playing computer games, or lost in some activity that you are interested in (it was reading when I was young). Hyperfocus leads outsiders to question the whole notion of whether the disorder exists: 'See, she can concentrate when she *wants* to, look at her transfixed in front of the telly – it's nonsense that she has ADHD.' Some scientists define interest as an emotion, and say that someone who loves a subject and becomes in the thrall of it can become hyperfocused on it. Hence why underachieving ADHDers may do well in certain subjects that they are really interested in, but not others, in a way that doesn't seem to fit in a pattern that parents or teachers spot.

---

[14] Hallowell, E and Ratey, J, *Answers to Distraction* (New York: First Anchor books, 2010).

Hyperfocus is still poorly understood and seems almost illogical – especially after you have just got your head around the idea that someone can't concentrate, and are now being presented with this concept of not being able to stop focusing on something. It helps if you think back to the description of ADHD as less of a "deficit of attention", and more of a "dysfunction of attention". Some scientists think it is dopamine related, that once an ADHDer gets stuck into something they enjoy, they find it difficult to come out of that state, to transition to something new, and a lack of dopamine causes that inability to shift gears. Kathleen Nadeau, a US psychologist, explains it in *ADDitude* magazine: *A better way to look at Hyperfocus [HF] is that people with ADHD have a dysregulated attention system. Like distractibility, Hyperfocus is thought to result from abnormally low levels of dopamine, a neurotransmitter that is particularly active in the brain's frontal lobes. This dopamine deficiency makes it hard to "shift gears" to take up boring-but-necessary tasks.*

The problems with hyperfocus occur when because of it the ADHDer fails to do all the other normal, important daily business, and misses deadlines and social interactions, or skips meals. In his book *Cyber Junkie* – ADHDer Kevin Roberts describes playing video games for twenty-two hours solidly, pretending to friends and neighbours that he was away for the weekend. Recently, a questionnaire was done on adult ADHD hyperfocus, offering the following definition: *A state of heightened, intense focus of any duration, which most likely occurs during activities related to one's school, hobbies, or "screen time" (i.e. television, computer use, etc.); this state may include the following qualities: timelessness, failure to attend to the world, ignoring personal needs, difficulty stopping and switching tasks, feelings of total engrossment in the task, and feeling "stuck" on small details.*[15] The work around the questionnaire provided strong scientific evidence that hyperfocus is an independent feature of Adult ADHD.

---

[15] Hupfeld, K.E., Abagis. T.R., Shah P, 'Living "In the Zone": Hyperfocus in Adult ADHD', *Atten Defic Hyperact Disord*, Jun;11(2), (2019), pp. 191–208.

In certain circumstances, hyperfocus can be an ADHD superpower. It is no accident that the most decorated Olympian in history, Michael Phelps, has ADHD, and has used his brand of hyperfocus to engage in a punishing training schedule that has contributed to his success (see page 91).

ACADEMIC ATTAINMENT

At the age of eighteen, it was an unhelpful lack of balance that tipped me over the edge, and this extreme hyperfocus, working from 6 am until 1 am every day, as well as depriving myself of sleep, didn't help me to get better grades at A-level. After the disappointment, I went on to university, committed to the idea that I would never "overwork" again. "Balance" was my new philosophy.

My final school report issued before my A-level results came out, which was the best I had ever received, with As in effort and progress for French, as well as the following prediction: *She should get a very good grade in the A-level.* Likewise, in Medieval History with a B double-plus: *I continue to be impressed by her essay-writing, which is of a high quality, and she has, furthermore, a sensitive understanding of the period. She deserves to do well.*

With predicted As for Russian as well, my kind Russian teacher Mr Adams wrote: *With very few exceptions, Emma's work this term has been at least good and at best excellent. She is still capable of astonishing follies (but aren't we all?), but these are now rare except under pressure.*

So, what happened next?

Never have teachers' predictions been so unanimously wrong. I got three Ds. Nobody could believe it, least of all me. Three Ds? Could that be right? My father said he was asking for a re-mark, he thought they had perhaps confused my result with that of my twin brother – cruelly known in the family as Dimmo Dommo, until he cracked this one with two As and a B. He was only allowed to take five GCSEs in total, whereas I had taken ten, and he wasn't even sure he would take more than two A-levels. Now he was bound for the London School of Economics. And my attempt at Oxbridge hung by a thread.

In a state of abject confusion, my whole identity had been staked on doing well, and after all my effort, I couldn't even claim to be too cool to work hard. I slumped emotionally and psychologically, not wanting to see anyone, not wanting to go out, and holed up in my room for weeks, sulking. I didn't want to talk to anybody about it because I didn't know what to say. I had revised by going into a state of hyperfocus[16], completely unbalancing myself by locking myself away in my room all day with my books, impervious to the call of the outside and probably proper food, and as I was at boarding school, there were no parents around to remind me to go to bed before 1 am. After all, what teacher or housemistress is going to tell a sixth-former to stop working so hard?

With the benefit of hindsight, I can see the combination of a poor working memory[17], mentioned by the ADHD psychiatrist in my diagnosis with reference to the A-levels, and anxiety about my performance in the exams, because I knew deep down my tendency to make those "astonishing follies", created a perfect storm. Back in my dramatic teens, I felt I had ruined my future.

CALL TO ACTION

Have you ever thought that your own or someone's ability to get lost in a project at work, school, or on the internet was evidence that they did not have ADHD? Could your new understanding of hyperfocus make you look again at yours or their interest, and see it as part of their inability to regulate their attention? What about underachievement in an otherwise bright child or person? Is this something you recognize in yourself or someone else? Could it be part of a personality puzzle that you have never quite put together?

---

16 Flippin, R., *What is ADHD hyperfocus?*, 2018 <https://www.additudemag.com/what-is-hyperfocus-add-video/> [accessed 4 August 2018].

17 Schweitzer, J.B., Hanford, R.B., Medoff, D.R., 2006. Working memory deficits in adults with ADHD: is there evidence for subtype differences? *Behav Brain Funct.* 2(43), (2006).

HOW TO RECOGNISE THE TRAITS OF ADHD

To qualify for diagnosis, the traits must not be explained by another mental disorder or expected developmental norms, but be shown as appearing in more than one setting (home and work/school) alongside evidence that symptoms interfere with or reduce the quality of functioning in a social or work/school environment.

Inattentive presentation: Six or more symptoms of inattention for children up to age sixteen, or five or more for adolescents aged seventeen and older, and adults:

1) Often fails to give close attention to details or makes careless mistakes in schoolwork, at work, or with other activities.
2) Often has trouble holding attention on tasks or play activities.
3) Often does not seem to listen when spoken to directly.
4) Often does not follow through on instructions and fails to finish schoolwork, chores, or duties in the workplace (e.g. loses focus, becomes side-tracked).
5) Often has trouble organising tasks and activities.
6) Often avoids, dislikes or is reluctant to do tasks that require mental effort over a long period of time (such as schoolwork or homework).
7) Often loses things necessary for tasks and activities (e.g. school materials, pencils, books, tools, wallets, keys, paperwork, eyeglasses, mobile telephones).
8) Is often easily distracted.
9) Is often forgetful in daily activities.

Hyperactive and Impulsive presentation: Six or more symptoms of hyperactivity-impulsivity for children up to age sixteen, or five or more for adolescents aged seventeen and older and adults:

1) Often fidgets with or taps hands or feet, or squirms in seat.
2) Often leaves seat in situations when remaining seated is expected.
3) Often runs about or climbs in situations where it is not appropriate (adolescents or adults may be limited to feeling restless).
4) Often unable to play or take part in leisure activities quietly.
5) Is often "on the go", acting as if "driven by a motor".
6) Often talks excessively.
7) Often blurts out an answer before a question has been completed.
8) Often has trouble waiting his/her turn.
9) Often interrupts or intrudes on others (e.g. butts into conversations or games).

Combined Presentation is six or more symptoms of both presentations from each list for children, and five of each for adults.

If you can count up to around five symptoms in two settings, i.e. home and work, for yourself or a loved one who may have ADHD, and think that it might be worth exploring a diagnosis, do bear in mind that only an ADHD psychiatrist or ADHD-trained nurse can diagnose someone in the UK, and you may want to ensure a similar medically trained person anywhere else in the world. People with ADHD are often said to have "poor self-regard", so we don't necessarily observe ourselves functioning as others do, so self-diagnosis is unreliable.

CHAPTER 3
SEEKING A DIAGNOSIS

"You may encounter many defeats, but you must not be defeated. In fact, it may be necessary to encounter the defeats, so you can know who you are, what you can rise from, how you can still come out of it."
Maya Angelou, poet

ADHD is often difficult to diagnose in the usual therapeutic situations, because the intensity of a therapist's room means the attention deficit doesn't always show up. The sufferer might be so engaged and focused in the exchange, that he or she doesn't seem capable of distraction at all, and so even those who have been able to afford therapy might not have hit upon the source of their difficulties in the counsellor's rooms.

The quiet of the therapist's room, the one-on-one attention, the lack of distracting factors – these influences can all help mask the usual distractibility and inattention. That's why the teacher at the coalface of the classroom environment (for a child), or partner (for an adult) is an important person to listen to – because *they see it daily*. Even therapists of adult ADHD sufferers have to be specialists, or must know what to look for, to recognise it in their client's lives; for example, the over-talkativeness won't necessarily be obvious where the client is encouraged to talk and the psychotherapist paid to listen.

Wherever you are in the world, the full ADHD assessment is a specialist examination, consisting of a structured interview (such as the DIVA 5.0) administered by a trained mental health professional, such as an ADHD nurse or a psychiatrist. In addition to the client describing his or her symptoms, a family member will be interviewed to confirm them. This process usually takes a minimum of 1–2 hours and is followed up by a report confirming or excluding the diagnosis. On the NHS in the UK, it will take considerably longer as there will be multiple screenings with an ADHD nurse before you finally get to meet the ADHD psychiatrist.

Adult ADHD is far more difficult to diagnoze than childhood ADHD, largely because the symptoms in isolation aren't unique to ADHD. Consultant psychiatrist Dr Judith Mohring explains that poor memory and concentration are common in depression and anxiety, for example, and struggling to function day-to-day is applicable to the vast majority of mental health conditions. The first interview and screening is so that the psychiatrist can rule out another diagnosis first that would better explain the symptoms.

This first assessment is usually a full psychiatric history. This explores the nature of the problems, how they began, how long they've been going on for, and anything that might be making the symptoms persist. In addition, the psychiatrist asks about any family history of mental health concerns, any physical health problems, and any medication taken (or drugs that aren't prescribed). "This first step takes anywhere from twenty minutes to an hour to explore," explains Dr Mohring, trained in DIVA 5.0, so any indication of a "first condition" has to be assessed and treated first before a short reassessment takes place. 'If there is a pattern of life-long difficulties with concentration, attention, impulsivity, and hyperactivity, which persists even now as an adult, the first problem is treated then a full assessment for ADHD takes place.'

I would recommend the private route if at all possible in the UK (and in other countries it may be your only route to diagnosis), especially if it is possible to have a "shared care" agreement with the NHS for medication subsequently, so you don't have to pay for it. For my own diagnosis, at the end of the three years that started with that initial visit to the GP, I had multiple screenings with an ADHD nurse and non-specialist psychiatrist. However, when it finally came to that one Wham-Bam-Thank-You-Ma'am kind of interview, it was the beginning of something new and exciting. The possibility of a better version of myself, perhaps, as this account from 17 January, 2016 suggests.

DIARY OF A DIAGNOSIS

My meeting with the NHS specialist ADHD psychiatrist Dr Jain took an hour and a half. It took place in a room with the ADHD specialist nurse, whom I had already met twice before being referred on to Dr Jain.

Dr Jain arrived with his wheel-on luggage, apologising for being late. I said it was a novelty for me not to be the one apologising, a start of a charm offensive that he was having no truck with. He barely looked up from his notes. Without a smile, he cleared his throat and began.

'Would your friends say that you talk too much, that you interrupt them when they are talking?'

Well, you'd have to ask them, I answered. I tried to explain that I didn't know if I talked too much, because I'm English, and that the English don't tend to tell you these things to your face.

No glimmer of humour from Dr Jain. 'Do you leave the table during dinner, or a film to get up and walk around?'

Not usually. I already wanted to offer layered answers, but there was no time. It was a simple 'Yes' or 'No'.

'Have you ever been fired from any jobs?'

Yes. I was fired in the summer from my first corporate job after just three months, I began to explain.

'How many jobs have you had?'

Dozens, but hadn't most journalists?

'What are your sleeping patterns?'

I don't seem to need as much sleep as most – I often go to bed after midnight and am up at 6 am most days.

'Would your partner/husband say that you argue a lot?'

Yes, probably.

'Have you tried any drugs?'

Yes, most when younger. Except heroin or crack cocaine.

'Which ones have you tried, specifically?'

I answered: cannabis, LSD, magic mushrooms, cocaine, ecstasy, MDMA.

He ticked them off the list, without asking when or how much or how often, or for how long. On and on the questions went. There was no time to give nuance, no time to explain the truth, to wonder out loud if that was the case, to remember, *even. This was like being in front of a firing squad, with questions raining like bullets down on me.*

By the end of the hour, our eyes were locked into that intense connection that sometimes happens when something important is going on. I've experienced this in therapy sessions, with a midwife when giving birth, when that helicopter pilot approached me after my son's road accident – "in the zone" as the Americans say.

'And what about as a child?' he asked. 'How was your experience of school?'

Good-ish. I was an academic scholar, but I was rebellious.

'What were your grades?'

Good for GCSE, but at A-levels I underperformed woefully and shocked everyone with three Ds after a prediction of three As.

'Were you in trouble much?'

Yes, a lot. I was "gated" thirteen times, when most pupils were usually suspended after two gatings, and expelled after suspension.

'Were you ever given responsibility?'

No, I was the only pupil doing seventh-term Oxbridge who wasn't made a prefect.

'Why weren't you expelled?' he asked.

Because I never did anything shockingly bad, just naughty.

'Did you sleep as a child?'

Only by rocking backwards and forwards seated in my bed for an hour or so, and then banging my head on the pillow. I even used to do this in my cot, apparently.

He looked over at the ADHD nurse. 'That's a new one,' he said.

He turned back to me. 'And what about games?'

Yes, I was very sporty. (I puffed up slightly – at last, something I could show off about!) I was in most of the school teams – volleyball, basketball, hockey, rounders, athletics, high jump and hurdles, cross-country.

'How did you get your scholarship?'

This was back in the day when it was awarded by a nod from the headmaster after doing well in an interview, I explained. I was only ten, and then I took an exam to transfer from the junior to the senior school.

'Did you daydream, or look out of the window?'

Yes, constantly. But I still managed to get ten GCSEs.

'What grades?'

One A, eight Bs, and a C.

'Where did you go to university?'

Exeter University, to read Russian and French, and I put my A-level disaster down to overworking. I learnt that extremes were not good for me. Balance *was. And I left university with a 2:1.*

Dr Jain wasn't interested in my philosophical meanderings. 'What about your relationships? Have you ever sought help for your relationships?'

Yes, often.

'How much therapy have you had over the marriage?'

About six years.

'Why so much?'

I felt like I needed it, I explained. And it worked. I'm still married, aren't I?

'Are you working now?'

Yes, I was back freelancing as a journalist since being fired from my corporate job in the summer. (I nodded over to the ADHD nurse who had tried to push through my diagnosis because she confessed later to seeing the writing on the wall. She had seen around 600 ADHD patients while in that job, and obviously saw me being fired way before I did.)[18]

And just like that, the interview was over.

I asked if a diagnosis was graded "mild", "moderate" or "severe" like it was in the new DSM (fifth edition).

'This is not America,' he said, 'We use different diagnostic material here[19]*. In the UK, and the NHS, you either have it or you don't have it.'*

So do I? Am I?

I waited, suspended for a moment as he flicked back through the notes, hiding behind his doctor's pad.

'Yes,' he answered definitively, not looking at me. 'Yes, you have it – the inattentive type, not the hyperactive type.' And then he reflected my life back at me in clinical, black-and-white terms.

---

[18] Bosely, S, *Undiagnosed adult ADHD could cost UK billions a year, report finds*, 2018 <https://www.theguardian.com/society/2018/feb/15/undiagnosed-adult-adhd-could-cost-uk-billions-a-year-report-finds> [accessed 2 August 2018].

[19] In UK and Europe – diagnosis of ADHD can be done using the World Health Organisation materials ICD-10, which refers to ADHD as Hyperkinetic Disorder and is marked by "early onset; a combination of overactive, poorly modulated behaviour with marked inattention and lack of persistent task involvement; and pervasiveness over situations and persistence over time of these behavioural characteristics".

'There are three main areas,' he described. 'Your relationship. The amount of therapy you have had is explained by the fact that the therapy wasn't working for you – it couldn't fix things.' Therapy has helped me enormously along the way: the support, the venting, the direction, the insight, I wanted to argue but he was not for being interrupted.

As for the jobs: the last unexpected sacking was an example of how I could underperform in my work.

And, finally, my academics. The unexpected grades for my A-levels. He said I could maintain my focus up to the GCSE standard, but at A-levels my working memory would have become more of a problem.

'So,' he summed up, 'from these three areas – relationships, academics and career – it's clear that you have it.'

As I left Dr Jain's room, I felt shell-shocked, eviscerated, vulnerable, open. The diagnosis wasn't the huge relief I thought it would be; I wasn't punching the air like I thought I would.

My life wasn't black and white, I realised; it was different shades of grey. And where was the positive, so much positive in a life well lived? I reflected.

I knew I had chosen to water the positive seeds, learnt to cultivate this side: the creativity, the love of people, empathy for the underdog, the new, challenging situations that some people abhor. *But was this just who I was? And not part of the ADHD? Where did I end and the ADHD begin?*

HOW TO SEEK A DIAGNOSIS

Getting a diagnosis can be relatively simple if done privately (simply pay an ADHD specialist psychiatrist £500+ after a referral from your GP here in the UK). However, if you decide to pursue a diagnosis on the NHS, be prepared for a long (and often) frustrating process. I took the NHS route because I wasn't in a rush to get a diagnosis. I had made it to aged fifty with the condition, so wanted to take some time to come around to the idea of even finding out I had it. So, I knew it would take a while, and it took three years.

PRIMARILY INATTENTIVE ADHD VERSUS SLUGGISH COGNITIVE TEMPO (SCT)

I am pleased to say that my diagnosis was primarily inattentive ADHD rather than SCT, for the vain reason that it is the most awful label. Sluggish Cognitive Tempo conjures up images of a giant mollusc leaving its slimy trail as it slowly creeps along, or paired with the word cognitive, implies a fancy name for just being plain stupid. It is, however, a different diagnosis – although it does have around 25% overlap with inattentive ADHD. Currently SCT is not included in any diagnostic manual, but will no doubt appear in the next DSM as the studies start to build. It refers to people who have both a tendency to daydream or space out, and have issues with feeling sleepy during the day. They are more likely to suffer from social withdrawal than their ADHD peers, who may experience rejection from their peers if hyperactive or impulsive.

Research has shown that roughly half of people scoring high for SCT don't meet the criteria for inattentive ADHD[20] so it is a discrete condition, and it is clear that more work needs to be done to bolster the seventy or so studies that include it. It is unassociated with the hyperactive/impulsive presentation, so is not associated with substance use disorder or oppositional defiant disorder or, worse, conduct disorder that can often lead an untreated ADHDer to end up in jail.

The best research is done by the expert Dr Russell Barkley, who offers a symptom threshold of five out of nine symptoms in his study of Adults with SCT. If this exists, along with impairment in one major life activity (such as work), an unofficial diagnosis can be made. Although Barkley has pinpointed cases of SCT in medical literature dating back to Alexander Crichton in 1798, his work on it is perhaps the most extensive to date. It can be treated with stimulant or non-stimulant medication, and is more significantly associated with depression than ADHD, so definitely deserves further research.

---

20 Hinshaw, S.P., Ellison, K, *ADHD: What Everyone Needs to Know*, (New York: Oxford University Press 2016).

SLUGGISH COGNITIVE TEMPO: VALIDATION IN ADULTS[21]

1. I am slow at doing things.
2. My mind feels like it is in a fog.
3. I stare off into space.
4. I feel sleepy or drowsy during the day.
5. I lose my train of thought.
6. I am not very active.
7. I get lost in my own thoughts.
8. I get tired easily.
9. I forget what I was going to say.
10. I feel confused.
11. I am not motivated to do things.
12. I zone out or space out.
13. My mind gets mixed up.
14. My thinking seems slow or slowed down.
15. I daydream.
16. I have a hard time putting my thoughts in order.

CALL TO ACTION

If you are interested in getting a diagnosis in the UK for yourself or a friend or family member, see a GP as early as possible to get a referral to an ADHD specialist. It is often recommended to take a close family member along if you are concerned about not being believed or being doubted in the few minutes that you have with the GP. ADHD is poorly understood, and not all GPs will be keen to make a referral if they don't quite believe the person presenting themselves has it. That's where the family member helps as back up. Even if you do decide to go down the private route at a later date, you will still need this first GP referral – so begin the process as quickly as you can, because it can take a long time.

---

21 Taken from the table 1.1 on page 7 of A review of Research of SCT by Dr Russell Barkley on his website www.russellbarkley.org

CHAPTER 4
HERITABILITY AND THE COMORBIDITIES

"Mental health is a state of well-being in which the individual realises his or her own abilities, can cope with the normal stresses of life, can work productively and fruitfully, and is able to make a contribution to his or her community."

World Health Organization, June 2015

Because ADHD usually runs in families[22], I can now see it in other members of my family. However, after my son was diagnosed, aged twelve, I spent a long time believing it was inherited from my husband's side. I even dragged my mother-in-law along to the 2013 International ADHD conference in Liverpool, thinking that she would have a light-bulb moment about her family's genetic contribution. However, it turned out to be my own light-bulb moment when, after chatting to a woman with ADHD, and playing "snap" with traits and coincidences that had persisted in our lives, I suddenly realised that it was *me* who perhaps had the ADHD after all.

Soon after, with the wool pulled away from my eyes, I could see it there in my dear father[23], to whom I am very close. My mother can recount endless stories of my father's unbelievable

[22] Twin studies enrolling many thousands of children around the world have shown that approximately 70–80% of the variability in the occurrence of ADHD is attributable to genetics (Gallo & Posner, 2016)

[23] 40% of all children with ADHD have at least one parent with the condition, this is consistent with the high heritability of ADHD (Barkley, 2008)

forgetfulness (he once reversed out of the drive to drop her at the train station, then sped off down the road, forgetting her altogether, leaving her to run desperately to the bus stop). Keys, passports, and wallets have been lost countless times, and when he once again lost his passport, leaving it on the seat of a taxi in Boston, my mother announced that she was never *ever* travelling abroad with him again.

As well as my father, there is his sister, my aunt – a very clever GP who has just celebrated her 80th birthday, and subsequently announced that she is getting married again (Go, girl!). My aunt has been married four times already, and earnt a state scholarship when young, allowing her to choose whatever university she wanted to attend in the country. She went on to become one of the first female GPs in this country to set up her own practice. At her son's 50th birthday dinner, when I mentioned the play on ADHD I was performing at the Edinburgh festival, she told me she thought that she had ADHD as well. Being a doctor, I believed her.

If ADHD is not caused by the more rare example of a brain injury or prematurity, then it is likely to be there, probably undiagnosed, somewhere in the family constellation. This is no small matter because it can lead to a kind of blindness of the condition, a normalising of family behaviour, which can limit the opportunities of diagnosis. All families are eccentric in their own way, but if you have ADHD parents and an ADHD child, or children, under the same roof together, there can be a lot more noise and drama than in the average suburban semi. As mentioned on page 7, 80% of ADHD is heritable, which is the same percentage as height, and there can be resistance to acknowledging it. If one family member has to own up to it, then the rest do, which is why so many adults come to it because of their child's diagnosis – up to this point, they have found coping mechanisms along the way to operate as the equivalent of a left-handed person in a right-handed world.

COMORBIDITIES

Comorbidities refer to an additional, co-existing condition that sits with the ADHD, often because of it, like depression or anxiety, or just out of coincidence. These might be learning difficulties, or Autism Spectrum Disorder (ASD) along with ADHD – although it must be emphasised that these are two completely different diagnoses. Then there are interesting connections, for example, around 50% of people who have dyspraxia or developmental co-ordination difficulties (DCD)[24], which affects how good you are at playing sports, for example, also have ADHD.

By far the most common comorbidities that co-exist with ADHD are anxiety and depression, which are probably caused by having the disorder. Given how the traits of restlessness, impulsivity, and distraction can impact on anyone's life, it is understandable how these two disabilities will arise. I have at various times, as a child, and during my adult life suffered from anxiety, but fortunately never depression. It appears that I sit in the statistical majority, the expert (but slight Eeyore of ADHD in my mind) Dr Barkley[25] estimates that 80% of adults with ADHD will experience at least one co-morbid condition in their lifetime, and you can see why some will turn to substance abuse to alleviate their symptoms[26], or tobacco[27].

DANGERS OF MISDIAGNOSIS

Interestingly, adults with undiagnosed ADHD are more likely to seek treatment because of problems associated with their comorbidities, such as anxiety or depression, than because of ADHD symptoms. This is a problem because certain

24 Watemberg N et al., 'Developmental coordination disorder in children with attention-deficit-hyperactivity disorder and physical therapy intervention', *Developmental Medicine & Child Neurology*, 49, no. 12 (2017), pp. 920–925.

25 Barkley, R.A., Murphy, K.R., and Fischer M, *ADHD in Adults: what the science says*. (New York: Guildford Press, 2011).

26 A nationwide study showed that, apart from any effects of pharmacotherapy with stimulants, approximately 15% of adults with ADHD (Kessler et al., 2006) have a comorbid alcohol/substance use disorder.

27 40% of people with ADHD smoke (ibid.,)

medications, such as Selective Serotonin Reuptake Inhibitors (SSRIs), are prescribed that work differently in ADHD neuroatypicals. In fact the psychiatrist Dr Jain who diagnosed me, pleaded with me to get the message out about ADHD to the wider public when he found out I was a journalist. He said that he dealt daily with patients who were referred to him after spending years and years in a bad way because they were on the wrong medication due to a misdiagnosis, because of a lack of understanding of ADHD.

More importantly, with depression and anxiety, some of the medication offered by doctors can actually be dangerous. 'Selective Serotonin Reuptake Inhibitors (SSRIs) help with affective, feeling anxiety,' says Dr Charles Parker, author of *The New ADHD Medication Rules.* 'But almost always make thinking/cognitive anxiety worse – they aggravate ADHD.' Without mincing his words in his book, published in 2010, Dr Parker goes on to write: 'SSRIs can make you crazy and make ADHD worse. *I repeat.* SSRIs can make pre-existing suicidal ideas much worse if the ADHD is not simultaneously treated.'[28]

SLEEP CONQUERS ALL

As well as the big-ticket comorbidities like depression and anxiety, there are also more under-the-radar problems going on in the ADHDer's life. Take sleep, for example. I had never thought about it much until the psychiatrist mentioned it during my diagnosis. In fact, the night-time was the time when I seemed to wake up more. I characterised myself as an owl, despite getting up with my lark-ish husband at 6 am regardless, and I never thought that the amount of sleep I was getting might thoroughly impact my day. Again, I am in the statistical majority of ADHDers.

'I don't know anyone with ADHD who does not have an issue with sleep,' says Dr Roberto Olivardia, a psychologist who treats ADHD at Harvard Medical School in the US. Olivardia explains

[28] Parker, C, *The New ADHD Medication Rules: Brain Science & Common Sense* (Virginia: Koehler Books, 2013), p. 48.

how vital sleep is to everyone, but especially to the person with ADHD if issues such as focus and concentration are at stake. We should all be getting our full eight hours, he lectures, and if the ADHD brain won't switch off to allow it, then it needs to be tricked into doing so, with all those clever sleep hygiene ideas that Sunday supplements tell us to do, including putting away the computer an hour before bedtime so the blue light doesn't make the body think it is daylight, having a relaxing bath, or using other night-time routines.

Olivardia also cites neurological research[29] that found that the 'ADHD brain is prone to a delayed sleep phase syndrome (DSPS).' Instead of having a typical circadian rhythm – with sleeping hours from 11 pm to 7 am like the rest of the world, an ADHD brain has an irregular pattern of 2 am to about 10 am, he says. This may explain why I often don't feel sleepy as the evening wears on, while my husband heads off to bed with his book by 11 pm. Armed with this knowledge, I have turned my sleep habits around to join him now, knowing that it is a wise idea.

Now I know that I should be getting eight hours sleep like everyone else, and that if I don't, I'm going to make my focus worse, I take long baths, or remind my husband to insist on giving me a hand up when he heads off to bed. I may not feel like going up, but forcing myself to start my bedtime routine like a toddler, rather than watch rubbish on the TV, is now my norm. 'Without enough sleep, ADHD medication treatment cannot work. Lack of sleep will wash out any treatment over time, often a very short time, and changes in meds won't work because the brain is fragged. Sleep is the best brain defrag, better than drugs, more effective than a vacation,' writes Dr Charles Parker.

Interestingly enough, my father, who has not really accepted that he may be the source of the heritable ADHD in the family, still prefers to fall asleep in front of the television and come up

---

29 Tartakovsky, M, 'Sleep Strategies for Adults with ADHD', *World of Psychology*, 2018, <https://psychcentral.com/blog/sleep-strategies-for-adults-with-adhd/> [accessed Sept 2018].

to bed in the early hours despite my mother's daily entreatment to do otherwise. I was asked by my ADHD nurse if I had tried "white noise" before I cleaned up my sleep hygiene to help get me to sleep earlier. I now realise my father is effectively self-soothing with the white noise of the television to lull him to sleep nightly.

However, bearing in mind that until 2008 ADHD in adults did not even exist in the UK, and children who turned eighteen were chucked out of child services and left to their own devices, you can see how much progress has been made in the last decade, and why people like my father have still to be brought up to speed. When I wrote this diary entry below about my son Michael, it not only had all the hallmarks of this family behaviour blindness (my usual stance of pushing the problem on to someone else: the nursery teacher, in this case), but also how I struggled to see how my child's behaviour was anything different from my own. I thought my throwaway line at the end was, just that. Only now can I reflect that this was written in 2005, three years before Adult ADHD even existed in the UK.

DIARY ENTRY: FRIDAY APRIL 10, 2005

I was greeted with a bombshell after the twins' fourth birthday party this week. Their nursery school teacher Mrs K, her of the perma-grin that delivers nothing but bad news, took me to one side and with her "gentle" bedside manner, in full audience of the other waiting mothers, tells me that she has 'grave concerns about Michael'. 'I'm thinking of getting him assessed by Special Needs for Attention Deficit Hyperactivity Disorder,' she says.

Fortunately, I recover from this baseball bat in the face sufficiently to ask her to hold fire for a moment. Yes, Michael is a "naughty boy", but there is nothing, well, "abnormal" about him, I argue.

It's true Michael doesn't like school, and he is so wilful that he will throw tantrums on demand when not getting his own way – but these are just the noisy facts of life, aren't they? He is also often the most loving and adorable of all of my three children, and the most thoughtful when he wants to be. That is obviously proof against ADHD, isn't it?

As I suffer tales of him tipping the books out of the book box, and then sitting in it ('No other child in the class has done this') and ripping books 'every day' (we had long ago renamed "lift-the-flap" books in our house as "rip-the-flap" books), I begin to wonder at his teacher.

'Can he hold a pencil yet?' I fire back, trying to put her on the back foot, and I immediately launched an enquiry into what he is actually learning in her class.

'I'm not worried about the academics at this stage,' she continues – deflecting, I thought, while deflecting myself – 'but he has been kicking the other children on occasions, and we have had to keep him back from going outside.'

Mean old witch! Surely that's the worst thing you can possibly do to an ebullient three-year-old?

I hate the feminisation of school, I railed inwardly, lots of goody-two-shoe women forever criticising small boys for not sitting quietly and obediently on a chair. Perhaps he'd do better in the run-around-the-hockey pitch private prep school method to tire him out. At least he wouldn't be a repressed, pent-up kid not allowed out of the class to run off steam when he's misbehaved.

Nonetheless, I am rattled at her words. I'll ask her to call off the Special Needs co-ordinator at this moment until after half term. The more I think about it, the more I realise that it is I, not Michael, who has ADHD. Coffee-fuelled, nicotine-craving, parking-ticket-waving, poor-excuse-of-a-wife-and-mother. That's it; it's time to change some patterns. Right here, right now. After this fag.

The point is, you may be able to rattle along quite happily in a slightly muddled and messy life – especially if you have the protective measure that I used to employ of blaming others for anything that went wrong. And for the 50% that might have problems with substance abuse, there are still 50% that don't, so different individuals will have different coping strategies. While I consider myself lucky to have escaped a lot of the pain that others suffer around this disorder, I am mindful that it comes for many with a whole lot of problems that aren't a one-off health issue, but a chronic underpinning of their lives.

FIVE NATURAL WAYS TO HELP DEAL WITH ADHD SYMPTOMS

Psychiatrist Dr James Arkell is a consultant psychiatrist at The Nightingale Hospital in London, and is an honorary lecturer at Imperial College London, who works with many patients who have ADHD amongst other diagnoses. Here he suggests some remedies and alternative therapies to help with the common side-effects of ADHD.

1) Magnesium chloride bath salts or skin oil are good to use in the evening, as are lavender oil capsules to aid sleep. There is small amount of research evidence for both products.
2) Some patients use a good quality CBD oil broad spectrum (with 0% THC) in the evening, also to aid relaxation and sleep. Proper evidence is not yet available.
3) Try to use a light lamp for twenty minutes in the morning to anchor your daily sleep rhythm and this will help with sleep issues in the evening.
4) Take broad spectrum micronutrients, which are now backed by nearly twenty years of independent research to help mood and anxiety-related disorders. They are expensive, but Hardy Nutritionals website has some useful videos on nutrition.
5) Use probiotics or save money and make your own kefir. There is some emerging evidence that healthy gut flora helps mood and attention.

TEN SAD FACTS ABOUT DEPRESSION AND ANXIETY

1) Between 9% and 50% of people with ADHD suffer from depression, depending on which of the studies[30] you look at.
2) Up to 25% of people with ADHD suffer from comorbid anxiety.[31]
3) One study[32] followed 123 young females with ADHD, alongside a control group of the same number for five years into early adulthood. Over 40% of the ADHD females had a major depressive disorder (MDD) compared to 11% of the control group.
4) Depression is one of the leading causes of disability and affects 264 million people, according to the World Health Organisation in 2020.
5) Depression and anxiety also costs the global economy $1 trillion a year in lost productivity, according to the World Health Organisation.
6) Among millennials (those aged 24–39), depression is the fastest-growing health condition, the Blue Cross Blue Shield Association recently found in 2020.
7) In a forthcoming survey from the charity Mind of 31,000 UK employees who reported having a mental health issue, 52% said they had experienced poor mental health at their current workplace.

---

30 McIntosh, D, et al., 'Adult ADHD and comorbid depression: A consensus-derived diagnostic algorithm for ADHD', *Neuropsychiatr Dis Treat*, 5, (2009), pp. 137–150.

31 Schatz, D.B., Rostain, A.L., ADHD with comorbid anxiety: a review of the current literature. *J Atten Disord*. 10(2), (2006) pp.141–149.

32 Biederman, J, Ball, S, Monuteaux, M, et al. New insights into the comorbidity of ADHD and major depression in adolescent and young adult females. *J Am Acad Child Adolesc* Psychiatry., 47, (2008), 426–434.

8) A 2019 poll by the American Psychiatric Association found 62% of people aged 20–37 feel comfortable discussing their mental health at work. Only 50% of those aged 54–72 reported the same in the survey.
9) Mind Share Partners surveyed 1,500 employees in 2019 – half of millennials and 75% of those aged under twenty-three had left a job in part because of mental-health reasons, voluntarily or involuntarily.
10) Almost 800,000 people die from suicide every year, and it is the second leading killer of young people aged 15–29.

CALL TO ACTION

Do you know someone who may be presenting with a comorbidity or a substance abuse disorder, which they find difficult to shake off? Perhaps they may have depression or anxiety that seems to be caused by a lack of ability to make progress in their lives, or a symptom of low self-esteem through constant job changes or failed relationships? Could these comorbidities be masking underlying ADHD?

CHAPTER 5
MEDICATION

"To people who say they don't believe in medication, I say: 'Medication is not a religion'."
Dr Edward Hallowell,
psychiatrist and author of *Driven to Distraction*

The final question the psychiatrist asked me at my diagnosis screening was: 'So … what do you want from me?'

'Medication,' I answered. 'If I need it.'

'The NHS diagnosis needs to establish that the ADHD is negatively affecting your life before you can qualify for the medication,' he explained.

"Impairment" is the technical term I have since learnt. Being a glass-half-full kind of person, I never thought of myself as a victim, or unlucky, or impaired in any way. So this was new territory for me. For the first time, I was silent. Awkwardly silent, as the diagnosis seeped in.

Dr Jain asked the nurse to take my blood pressure – it was high. 'I can't give you medication if your blood pressure is so high,' he said, shaking his head. This shook me out of my stupor. My blood pressure was usually normal, but I had just been giving a life-changing diagnosis, so I took a few deep breaths and asked for it to be taken again on the other arm. It was a stressful experience being questioned this way. I just needed a moment to breathe. This time the blood pressure was lower.

'Okay,' he said. 'We'll try you on Equasym XL [a stimulant like Ritalin with the active ingredient methylphenidate hydrochloride].

It's an eight-hour stimulant. Start with one a day for a week, and then up it to two a day by two weeks. Then we'll see you in two weeks' time to see how you are doing.' He held out the prescription.

'Would my personality change?' I asked.

'No, you'll just be able to concentrate better.'

Later my husband wouldn't believe this. He said he didn't want me to lose my sense of humour, become all "stern". 'I like you the way you are,' he said, rather sweetly. 'Personality is a complicated thing,' he argued, 'put you on meds and it could change.'

Despite pleading my case with the psychiatrist Dr Jain to have access to ADHD medication, I had been completely opposed to all forms of ADHD medication just a few years earlier. When my son Michael was diagnosed, aged twelve, the psychiatrist told me, in front of the teachers, that the first line of treatment on offer was Ritalin (methylphenidate). I shook my head and said I wouldn't ever consider this. I was adamant that no child of mine would take psychoactive drugs. Now, here I was, asking for them for myself. How could such a *volte-face* happen in such a short space of time?

By the time of my own diagnosis a few years later, I realised that people with ADHD who don't take medication are often in danger of self-medicating (see Chapter 6) with nicotine, caffeine, cannabis, alcohol, and even cocaine. On the surface, some may argue caffeine, alcohol, and nicotine are better than taking a mind medication, but such people also need to be reminded that cannabis and cocaine are illegal, expensive, mixed with other harmful products, and unregulated. For example, Britons are among the highest consumers of cocaine in Europe, with the OECD reporting that Brits consume more than double the European average, despite its links to violence, slavery, and organized crime. So why then is there is so much stigma around taking a medication that is safe enough to give to children, has been used since the 1930s, and has undergone numerous medical trials to be prescribed at a specific dosage to an ADHD sufferer?

I think it has as much to do with my husband's worry about a personality change – knowing that strong doses of ADHD medication can produce such a calming effect on a child, adults might worry that their natural zest for life might be dampened, making them become unrecognisable. The purpose of medicating ADHD children is so that they can become focused enough to learn some helpful routines and life skills, as well as something at school, that they can carry on with whether on medication or not. The same is true for adults, who also need to use the medication to habituate better daily habits, such as keeping their living and work spaces in order, tackling boring tasks, and setting up routines so things are not lost.

Like drinking a big cup of coffee can motivate you to settle down and tackle a project you've been putting off, the medication also wears off, but after a number of hours rather than minutes. It can be used for days when you need it, it can be used at a lower dose than the recommended prescription if you need it to just to keep you working on a project – rather than procrastinating about starting it. Medication for ADHD is usually a relatively short-acting stimulant, it doesn't have to be a take-it-and-change-for-ever potion of Alice in Wonderland description. And there is a dizzying array of different types, so experimenting with dosage and brands are vital.

TYPES OF ADHD MEDICATION

ADHD medication has a multitude of different names and brands, but basically falls into two categories: short-acting stimulant medication and long-acting non-stimulant medication. Short-acting means it doesn't last long, or stay in your system for long; long-acting means that it takes time to build in your system, sometimes over weeks, and doesn't wear off in the same way.

STIMULANTS

The first type, the stimulant medication, is often referred to as Ritalin because this was an early brand name. People find it hard to get their head around the idea of giving a stimulant medication to someone who is already pretty "bouncy", a term often used for the challenging ADHD children in our classrooms.

It seems counter-intuitive. Why would you give "speed" to a child or adult who is already speedy? In basic terms, for example in the classroom, if you are lacking in the chemical dopamine, in order to make things a bit more interesting and stimulating for yourself you might tap the desk, swing on your chair, flick your pen back and forward, jiggle your leg, chatter incessantly, ask questions – pretty much anything other than sit quietly and get on with what's in front of you (unless you absolutely love the subject). That is what an ADHD child without stimulant medication can behave like.

A stimulant medication raises that child's dopamine levels, which are lower in those with ADHD than in others, so they no longer need to "self-stimulate" (tap the desk, swing on their chair, lob paper balls at the person in front etc.). As the child experiences the same dopamine levels as others, he or she then finds that they can focus on the task in front of them.

The biggest side-effect of stimulant medication is a suppressed appetite, so those who take it may need to get in the habit of eating despite not feeling particularly hungry. This is no bad thing if eating is one of your ways of self-stimulating as an adult, and you perhaps have the mid-life paunch to show for it.

Caffeine is also a stimulant, and I find it helpful to think of the stimulant medication as a coffee/caffeine hit; it may also help some reduce the feeling of stigma around taking medication. These stimulant medications are not prescribed lightly; they are "controlled drugs" because they can be addictive if taken by people who do not have ADHD. You may have read about the scandals in the US of ADHD medication being traded by college students to help them study longer, and this form of abuse can lead to addiction. Stimulant medication is not addictive to those who have ADHD.

NON-STIMULANTS

The other form is non-stimulant medication, such as Atomoxetine, which takes up to a week to two weeks to take effect in one's system, and works on the brain chemical norepinephrine. It is given to those who don't like the side-effects of the stimulant medication, such as loss of appetite or insomnia, in some cases, as well as those people with ADHD for whom stimulants don't work. Some of the non-stimulant medication also treats depression, so may be offered to those who suffer comorbidities such as anxiety or depression with their ADHD. Non-stimulant medication also comes with a bunch of side-effects.

In my adult ADHD WhatsApp group, a noisy but caring rabble who post up to 200 messages a day, many of them instantly deleted, newbies to medication are invited to join a breakout group for those on long-acting stimulants for a more 'peaceful vibe'. This usually prompts a barrage of pestering by the group to ask if they can join as well, until a hundred messages later they have forgotten what they wanted to join.

To find the right medication, the best way is to experiment with different brands or doses after diagnosis. If you still don't like the idea of taking medication, then, as the next chapter shows, there is still plenty that can be done to alleviate symptoms, including exercise and diet. The main priority is to educate yourself, and find other ways of managing the disorder. I would never suggest someone tries medication without a diagnosis, but I have sat in on an adult ADHD seminar where one of the top experts who has ADHD (and who will remain nameless) explained that the fastest route to finding out whether you had the condition or not was to try the medication. If the medication works, and suddenly you experience the calm and focus that you have always craved, then you have it.

Someone piped up in the room to remind the American visitor that here in the UK the supply or possession of a Class B drug, such as Ritalin, carried a maximum penalty of five years in prison[33] and an unlimited fine, or both. 'Perhaps not such a good idea to say that I suggested that,' backtracked our American expert quickly. 'Forget I ever said that!'

---

33 GOV.UK,'Drug Penalties', <https://www.gov.uk/penalties-drug-possession-dealing> [accessed September 2018].

MEDICATION FOR MY SON

In order for me to rationalise the eventual decision to give my son medication, which was made after he was suspended from school and I was suddenly facing the prospect of home-schooling him, I had to find a way to justify it to myself. As mentioned earlier, I had spent a year not giving him medication after his diagnosis because I was violently opposed to the idea. Now, with the help of a specialist psychiatrist, I was beginning to understand why the alternative was worse. First, I had to stop referring to medication as "drugs" with all the red-top tabloid associations of low-lifers jacking up in hallways that it might suggest. This required me to turn all my preconceptions around drugs – both legal and illegal – on their head. Despite the need for society to classify them in a certain way, the idea that there is some moral aspect to drugs – recreational are bad, medicinal are good, those who take Class A drugs deserve prison, those who take Class Cs, don't – are nonsense when I began to look deeper into the subject.

Instead of feeling a failure as a mother, angry about a system that couldn't contain a child like Michael, as I had done for a year after his diagnosis, I began to look at it differently and realise that this had less to do with me and more to do with improving his life chances. With the immediate miraculous turnaround in his behaviour after giving him medication, he could be back in school on day two of taking it. That meant he was back with his social group, mixing with his peers, and learning how to exist within a boundaried world where he suffered consequences if he broke rules.

Then, after a number of weeks on the medication, it was clear his natural intelligence was beginning to shine through in his school work, even if his sparkiness was a little subdued. The immediate trade-off was between how he felt about himself as he was out of the system, discarded and excluded by his peers, versus his self-esteem as he began to start to do well. On medication, he was suddenly able to concentrate in class, and although he still reverted to calling out and forgetting to put his hand up at times, teachers reported in his weekly Conners assessments[34] that his grades and attitude were improving.

Up until Michael started medication, aged thirteen, I had left most parents' evenings in tears. Sometimes, I felt my eyes watering while sitting opposite the teachers, even as they started their appraisal with a big sigh and a smile, and an attempt at a good-humoured and positive beginning. I think I transformed from parent into child at those hated parents' evenings. The more I sat opposite the teachers to listen to them talk about Michael's behaviour, the more I heard my own schooldays discussed, where I clearly struggled with authority – and often I found myself challenging the teachers' opinions as an adult.

Even the teachers that were Michael's champions, such as his maths teacher Mrs Griffiths, seemed to reduce me to tears when they marshalled all their resources to tell me only the good things that they found in his work. I found the parents' evenings so stressful, that I used to urge my husband to go instead, or do them with me, and I would sit uncharacteristically silent throughout.

But that all changed the term Michael began medication. For the first time, we were discussing his grades in an exam – or how he had turned in a good piece of homework – it all felt optimistic. It was like a revelation, and I even felt better about attending on my own. My stubbornness about accepting medication was rooted as much in all the headlines around it, phrases like: "chemical cosh" or "Ritalin kids". It was a fear of change. But now I had crossed that divide and showed up on the other side, I wondered why it had taken me so damn long.

Now all I had to weather was other people's disapproval when they told me: 'I don't believe in giving children drugs.' ADHD psychiatrist and author Dr Hallowell advises responding to the "I-don't-believe-in-drugging-children" brigade, with: 'You don't have to believe in it. Medication is not a religion.' I am also careful never to refer to "drugs", with all its illegal connotations, and insist

---

34 Conners ratings scales (CBRS) include a form for teachers to fill out, to give feedback to a doctor or psychiatrist about a child's response to medication.

on calling it "medication". I know the power of words having worked in the media.

So, just as the medication thyroxine has kept my mother alive since her thyroid collapsed thirty years ago, so the medication for ADHD deserves similar recognition. Just because it affects the mind, not the body, shouldn't add stigma. The controversy around medication, especially for children, spoke to me of how society's conditioning was to see the invisible neural failings as moral ones: calling ADHD 'laziness', 'lack of effort', or 'naughtiness', rather than understanding that it was a biological deficiency, a lack of dopamine in the neural pathways. Until mental health is given the same weight as physical health, this won't change. Meanwhile, Michael on medication was, ironically, like a religious conversion. And if this was a religion, I was a convert.

MEDICATION FOR ME

Seeing Michael begin to flourish in school academically meant that by the time of my own diagnosis, I was ready to see if I could also experience a similar transformation. The piles of clutter on my desk, late tax returns, and general disorganisation were hardly a wasted life, but nevertheless they were drowning my ability to get on with the important business of finishing projects.

There was also the internal chattering and self-recrimination when my day would start unintentionally at 11 am, not 9 am, because I had got distracted with some pressing, non-urgent domestic issue, or was hunting around looking for a charger/scissors/parking fine. Once on medication, I would look up from my desk having started work on time, to find that only twenty minutes, not two hours had passed, perhaps because I hadn't descended down some internet rabbit hole, hung up on a piece of research that would be cast aside shortly because it was fascinating, but had nothing to do with the story I was working on.

On medication, I would arrange to interview or speak to people and call them on the dot, rather than be running around the house looking for the phone at the time I was due to call. Piles of stuff, shoved into cupboards for the "rainy day" sort out, were lifted out and miraculously sifted through, with things casually thrown into the bin (rather than being hoarded on a "maybe" pile, and then shoved back in the cupboard again when they toppled over later). It wasn't just the ability to focus – somehow the emotion had gone out of such daily chores. Whole narratives that I had invented in my head, similar to the stories I told myself around smoking, disappeared with the medication.

Then there was the emotional calming. Whereas before medication, I might be thrown off track for the rest of the day by an unpleasant encounter that then threatened to ruin my day, such as finding out a bill had doubled during my long procrastination period, or by seeing a photo of someone I had since fallen out with, I now dealt with these distractions or put them to one side, rather than letting them lead to a flurry of pointless activity to somehow suppress the uncomfortable feelings.

The main downside to the meds was that sometimes my newfound zealousness meant that I would tackle in too intense a manner the chores that had been left slumbering for a lifetime, so that as I cleared my desk, I would notice a wardrobe in need of a trip to the charity shop, and soon I would be folding up old clothes to take into town rather than working. Cleaning and clearing up the house was in danger of becoming a whole new distraction, despite the obvious pleasure at the prospect from a disbelieving family. However, I didn't want them getting any ideas, and I wasn't about to turn into a lobotomised extra from *Valley of the Dolls*, so I checked this tendency in the mirror, and took to purposely leaving a bit of kitchen clutter to pile up.

WILL THE MEDICATION CHANGE MY PERSONALITY?

Fears that the medication will cause a personality change is a common concern. I had to weigh this up against the big-ticket items in life, like money, which never lasted long in my account, and moving house or jobs constantly – with medication came the chance to make changes. And for someone diagnosed so late, this was a double-edged sword. Psychoactive medication is controversial for a good reason – personality is a complex thing. Do you want to become instantly calmer, more focused, or seemingly "boring" (to yourself)? Thomas E. Brown, ADHD specialist, equates using medication with wearing glasses; you will never cure the ADHD, but with the glasses on, you can see better.[35]

Michael's twin sister says he is less fun on his medication, so during the holidays he doesn't take it. This may mean things are a lot noisier, and there are more fights and drama with the others in the family, but Michael's energy means that he is also able to find jobs and still go out and party. Now, at aged nineteen, he doesn't see the need to take the medication unless he has to do something that requires concentration, like studying. He took it with him on his gap year travels, but never used it.

Currently writing this under lockdown for the coronavirus, I attempted to set up the structure missing from us all being thrown back together again as the twins were recalled from the other side of the world from their gap year. Michael's decision not to take medication sometimes makes life at home more challenging for the rest of the family. Mealtimes of lunch and dinner, observed as the bare minimum of family unity, often became a prodding match as Michael would swivel his gaze at who he could wind up as he lobbed a verbal hand-grenade into the middle of the table. ADHD in lockdown across the country cannot have been a pretty sight – and it takes real maturity not to melt down into dramas and keep things positive. Would Michael being on medication have been helpful for the rest of the family at this time? Yes, probably. However, we live in an imperfect world – and if nothing else, this virus has been sent to show us that with bells on.

I have continued to take half my dose of medication during lockdown, because I felt I needed to offer that less volatile presentation of myself, keeping some structure to the day for the rest of the family. My motive was different to when I first started taking medication, which began to open up a world of possibilities. Medication doesn't totally conquer the distractibility, and generally

---

35 Brown, T.E., *Outside the Box: Rethinking ADD/ADHD in Children and Adults: A Practical Guide* (Arlington: American Psychiatric Association Publishing, 2017), p.143.

I only take half of the prescribed dose anyway so that I can still feel like myself, but I am a more joined-up version of myself. And as the bills got paid, and I wrote down my many passwords and tackled my tax return, tackled "the pile", a certain peace descended.

TIME BLINDNESS

On medication, everything feels doable. For example, I experienced for the first time being early for events, I was no longer "time blind". That feeling, I learnt, keeps the anxiety at bay. And it doesn't necessarily mean the fun is over.

Overall, easily the strangest aspect of being on ADHD medication is what happened to my concept of time. I had no idea how time can be experienced by others, because all my life "time" has been this thing that can run away without me noticing. With the busyness of distraction, my husband always accused me of "leaving the house at the time you are expected to arrive somewhere". Once on medication, I began to arrive early, because time was something that seemed to have magically expanded. I rather enjoyed the experience of being able to prepare or plan, instead of rushing headlong into situations. Medication brought with it a wholly new relationship with time.

For the first time ever, I would sit in a car park experiencing an odd pleasure that I had arrived early for something – literally a novelty. Far from feeling wrong, I began to enjoy being early, watching events being set up around me, having a coffee before I read the press pack if on a work assignment, doing interviews before everyone got too busy, as opposed to my usual dashing in when the thing had already started.

On medication, this drastic sense of time disappearing also vanishes. I look at the clock and miraculously it is not a whole hour later than I thought it was, but the minute hand has barely moved. It's weird, but it's weird in a good way, because I don't need to speed to get somewhere in the car, or construct apologies on arrival. It feels a strange, unknown sensation. How can it all be that simple when I have struggled all my life to be anywhere on time?

HELPFUL FACTS ABOUT ADHD MEDICATION

By psychiatrist Dr James Arkell (see page 55).

In the UK there are two stimulants and it is often worth adults with ADHD trying out both of them at different times to evaluate which suits one better in terms of side-effects and effectiveness. The basic ingredients are either methylphenidate (brand names: Equasym, Ritalin, Tranquilyn, ConcertaXL or Medikinet) or dexamfetamine.

The medications mainly act on the two main neurotransmitters that are often deficient in those with ADHD: dopamine (associated with drive and goal focus) and noradrenaline (associated with energy). Methylphenidate slows the reuptake by the nerve endings and so there is a more ambient transmitter, while dexamfetamine increases the amount released.

When it comes to treatment, it's a bit like Goldilocks and the three bears with her porridge; the dose can be "too little, too much or just right". Adults sometimes prefer the cheaper immediate release version as it gives more control and flexibility in dosing, whereas for children it can be more practical to give them one long-acting dose in the morning and send them to school. You need to be your own expert on how it affects you in the day. For example, a solicitor may want to be on stimulants in the morning to go over data-heavy documents, and off it to meet clients in the afternoon. If you have anxiety or depressive symptoms, then these need to be treated and stable first, before adding stimulants carefully.

With both dexamfetamine and methylphenidate the raw stimulants often need to be taken more than once a day to benefit for the whole working day, and with both medications there are different, more costly branded preparations available that are longer acting and can be taken just once in the morning. The common slow release methylphenidate capsules are Concerta XL and Medikinet. Elvanse capsules contain lisdexamfetamine that the liver slowly digests into dexamfetamine throughout the day, so it doesn't need to be taken more than once.

The alternative common non-stimulant medications are atomoxetine, bupropion, and guanfacine. These are usually taken if the stimulants are not successful or appropriate.

CALL TO ACTION

The decision to take medication is a personal one, and should be separate to seeking a diagnosis or educating yourself around ADHD. However, if you don't explore or try medication, look carefully at whether some form of self-medication is taking place in your life via the back door instead? Do you consume alcohol, tobacco or even illegal drugs, often when those around you have seemingly "grown out" of those habits? Would knowing that taking a safe, well-researched ADHD medication may help control this form of more harmful self-medication, or stop its usage altogether, change your opinion about how you view ADHD medication as a "bad thing"? After all, is, say, tobacco, alcohol, cannabis or cocaine really better for you?

CHAPTER 6
SELF-MEDICATION

"The devil has put a penalty on all things we enjoy in life. Either we suffer in health or we suffer in soul, or we get fat."

Albert Einstein

One of the stranger questions that I didn't expect to be asked during my diagnosis was a fast history of my recreational drug use. What did that have to do with anything? Then, as I began to self-educate, I started to see the connection. Dopamine. Dope. Surely the two are related? Dopamine is lacking in people with ADHD, so where is the best place to find it? In dope, of course. Dope yourself up to get the extra dopamine. There are hundreds of studies to confirm this – that cannabis is the preferred self-medication for those with ADHD, and that substance use disorder (SUD for short) has been proven to be not just a young person's thing, but something that can carry on into late adulthood.

Until 2008, in the UK, ADHD was deemed only a childhood disorder, and ceased to exist after the age of eighteen, so it is only relatively recently that scientists have started researching the adult population. The result was predictable. Even after the age of twenty-five, generally thought to be the end of adolescence, those with ADHD are still partying on regardless.[36] While the rest of the population are hanging

[36] Osland, S, Hirsch, L, Pringshelm, T, 'Smoking, alcohol and drug use in youth and adults with attention-deficit hyperactivity disorder'. *BJ Psych Open*. 3 (3) (2017), pp. 141–146.

up their dancing shoes, ADHDers are still looking for ways to increase their fix of dopamine. If it isn't racing cars, or becoming skydivers, it is likely to be taking illegal drugs. As Thomas E Brown explains, as those suffering from ADHD are lacking in certain brain chemicals, it's perhaps unsurprising to find that they make up for it with continued experimentation with other chemicals.

When the appeal began to fade for most, as they grew up and got ahead in the career stakes, or were felled by child-rearing, then alcohol in general and wine in particular, became the socially acceptable drug of choice. Anything else becomes something of an unacceptable proposition. And so the person with ADHD might find themselves falling in with a younger, or more unsavoury crowd. Or perhaps hiding somewhat shamefully their dependence on other substances to keep them on track.

What I never understood when I was younger was why many of the drugs I experimented with didn't seem to affect me in the same way as they did other people. And because I didn't fully trust myself around drugs, because I observed that they didn't seem to affect me in the same way, I was always slightly anxious around taking them. Quite often the drug everyone was taking would have the opposite effect on me. Not many people, for example, have fallen asleep after taking cocaine, feeling strangely calm, or had the kind of terrifying experience on the euphoric drug of clubber's choice Ecstasy that I have.

Take MDMA or Ecstasy, for example (or don't it if you haven't tried it before). At the beginning of the 1990s, it was considered a lounge lizard experience, with everyone sitting around talking meaningfully about feelings and emotions, able to emote without the usual British awkwardness, or snogging away on the sofa with someone they had just admitted they fancied. For my boarding school generation, people opened up about their sexuality, came out as gay, told each other they loved each other; and one couple even got engaged after taking it. The MDMA powder, a purer form of the pill to follow, was touted at the time as being originally designed for marriage counselling[37].

As Ecstasy moved to become a drug for clubbers, it morphed into little pills with names such as "white doves", "disco biscuits", and "rhubarb and custard" that were cut with other chemicals, to make the pill poppers dance, and to make music that was barely tolerable sober seem like suddenly the most euphoric beats in the world. The higher the beats per minute, and the less vocals, the better. The music was designed to track the "rushes" of the drug, with DJs "building their set" and then releasing the robotic clubbers into an ecstatic trance-like state, everyone waving their arms madly as if they had just reached nirvana. I found the tribal, sweaty club scene and house music difficult to understand until I listened to it on E. Then it all suddenly made sense.

However, what went up also came down – and this I found difficult to take. The comedowns were frightening to me in their intensity, so I would mostly pretend to take the pill just to be out with the crowd. I would take a nibble and hide the rest, or throw it away. On it, I often felt far too out of control from the roller-coaster effect, particularly as it began to wear off, when just one casual comment could make me feel like I was plummeting down into an abyss, which felt visceral in its pain.

The intensity of the downward falling, like a nightmare, meant that what lingered for me was the memory of the comedown – and not the coming up. And then the coming up was muddled with the coming down, or the fear of coming down rather than the actual coming down, because I was worried that something might happen that would break the spell. This fear was fomented after one night in Ibiza, when I experienced the complete flipside to the drug; a giant comedown when, after witnessing a car crash on the way back from a club at 6 am, the roller-coaster did not stop descending. The pills hadn't worked that night, but when we

---

[37] Gander, K, *Love, sex and MDMA: could the party drug be used for couple's therapy?*, 2016, <https://www.independent.co.uk/life-style/love-sex/mdma-sex-relationships-couples-therapy-can-it-work-a7349836.html> [accessed 18 August 2018].

got home, it suddenly took hold of me. The image of the girls bleeding on the roadside flooded my whole mind, and I couldn't get rid of it. I felt racked by a heart-wrenching guilt about not going in the ambulance with the girls, the sight of leering men as they stood up dazed and confused, and the more I worried, the worse I felt. Eventually it began to feel as if my own heart and entrails were lying on the bed next to me as I struggled to stay calm and breathe through this interminable negative "rush". Instead of going up on that E, I went down, right down, and it took hours for this painful feeling to wear off. After that, I never wanted to take it again.

If taking Ecstasy felt like an unpleasantly intense trip that could flip, then cocaine seemed to have little effect whatsoever. If I did ever take it, the euphoric chattiness that everyone else seemed to enjoy would have the opposite effect on me. I'd experience strange teeth-grating, probably from whatever it was cut with, and then would remain like silent prey to whomever needed to get their story out. If anything, I would feel "straighter" than I had before I had taken it; the effect of the wine might wear off, and I felt almost ready to do a crossword. I remember taking it at a party once and being described by someone who didn't know me as a "placid" person – not a usual description of my personality.

Of course, now I know it is a stimulant, and therefore, like the Ritalin that is administered medically, I understand why it calms rather than hypes up an ADHD brain. It's why so many undiagnosed are drawn to this kind of substance abuse, to self-medicate with it. Because ADHDers on stimulants slow down, the dopamine-deficient neurotransmitters and receptors are nourished, and the brain feels like it's operating optimally. No need to fidget to get your dopamine fix or drive fast when it is delivered through cocaine.

I also was scared of hallucinogens, and didn't like the idea of being out of control on LSD or magic mushrooms. When I did try them, I only liked the day after, when I knew it was over and I had a strange sense of feeling free in my body. While I was on it, I just wanted to be off it, anxious that I might never "come down", and so fought the experience. At some point I would sit with my head in my hands in a loo cubicle, willing it to be over.

While I was too scared to dabble in the opiate trap of really heavy drugs, such as heroin, crack or methamphetamine, a few of my friends in the 1980s did. If you hang out with people who take illegal drugs, then problems happen. I can count on more than one hand those who died young in my group of friends, because addiction led to overdose. For those who may have been ADHD themselves, because like seeks out like, it is a reminder how this neurological condition can be a killer.

TAKING DRUGS OR SELF-MEDICATION?

Now with the understanding that other forces may have been at work, such as redressing a chemical brain imbalance, I no longer see drug-taking as some moral failing. Taking medication has helped me to see it as a form of self-medication. Diagnosis has encouraged me to look at how to quit destructive behaviours for good – particularly nicotine, which I have struggled with for the longest. After diagnosis, and taking medication, and realising that some of the difficulty I had quitting smoking may have been related to the ADHD, I decided to use the NHS stop smoking service to access a nicotine-inhibiting medication called Champix, to stop the habit. It works because it binds to the nicotine receptor in your brain, and stops the brain craving nicotine. So, I literally forgot about smoking. This was a wholly different experience to my usual attempts to quit, all thirteen of them, where I would make up whole narratives around why I deserved just one cigarette, after feeling wretched and depressed for the first few weeks.

Quitting with Champix was relatively easy, not least because it came with a service where you checked in with a health professional weekly, who kept you on track and made you blow into a nicotine inhaler to check that you had not been smoking. There were some fairly strange side-effects to Champix, such as intense and hyper-real dreams, and some of the chat rooms around this medication have hair-raising stories of people committing violent acts on their spouses, or driving unaware for miles, but my side-effects were fortunately just intense, vivid dreams.

Now I have a completely different understanding of drug-taking, and an open-mindedness towards challenging the orthodoxy surrounding it, especially imprisoning people for relatively minor drug offences. If you were to substitute the word "drug" for "medication", and therefore ask the question whether the person might be self-medicating, instead of taking drugs, would that change the way you might consider some of their "crimes"? It might encourage society to see the cost of locking up those who fall foul of the law, wasting lives, breaking up families, needlessly stopping research into these illegal substances because they are viewed as part of a moral problem. We have a long way to go, because there is still a moral majority who want to believe that they are above this type of person, without acknowledging that legal intoxicants and psychoactive substances such as alcohol and tobacco often cause far more harm in society, especially through drink driving, domestic abuse or early death from lung cancer.

ADHD AND SUBSTANCE USE

According to the diagnostic manual DSM-5 (see page 35), "substance related disorders" include ten classes of substances: alcohol, amphetamines, caffeine, cannabis, cocaine, sedatives, tobacco, inhalants (like butane or glue), opioids, and hallucinogens, and "all drugs that are taken in excess have in common direct activation of the brain reward system"[38].

It is perhaps not surprising to learn then that there are thousands of studies showing the relationship between ADHD and substance use. Studies that show, for example, that adults who have had a lifetime of substance abuse are likely in 25% of cases

---

[38] American Psychiatric Association, *Diagnostic and Statistical Manual of Mental Disorders, 5th edn (DSM-5)* (Washington D.C.: American Psychiatric Publishing, 2013).

to have ADHD, a far higher incidence than its occurrence in the adult population (7–8%).

Some scientists, such as Ovide F. Pomerleau[39], have looked at particular substances such as tobacco, and discovered that during the late 1990s, 40% of adults with ADHD smoked against a general population of only 26%. Others noted that ADHD has a significant association with the early onset of cigarette smoking.[40]

As ADHDers move from adolescence to adulthood, the rates of substance use rapidly increases compared to neurotypicals, as does the length of time they continue to use substances, with the average duration being 133 months compared to 95 months between the ADHD versus non-ADHD groups.

ADHD AND ADDICTION

What isn't examined in much detail is the cause of substance use in ADHDers. Some studies cite reducing the symptoms of hyperactivity, impulsivity, and restlessness, but that doesn't necessarily explain some of the substances that are being consumed, such as alcohol. It is not as simple as just saying ADHDers are self-medicating, because something more complex is going on around addiction, as well as the emotional effect of ADHD – and those comorbidities of anxiety and depression (see page 50).

Perhaps the most important conclusion of many of the studies is that they show that the legal stimulant medications, such as Ritalin, that might resemble illegal substances such as cocaine but have a slower uptake in the brain, do not add to the risk of substance abuse in those with ADHD. If anything, there is evidence that there is a *reduction* in risk of substance abuse for younger people treated with legal stimulants, used as prescribed. Most research suggests that the stimulant pharmacotherapy appears to decrease SUD by as much as one half – a significant

---

39 Pomerleau, O.F., et al., 'Cigarette smoking in adult patients diagnosed with ADH'. *Journal of Substance Abuse* Volume 7, Issue 3, 1995, pp. 373–378.

40 Milberger, S, Biederman, J, Faraone, S.V., Chen, L, Jones, J,. ADHD is associated with early initiation of cigarette smoking in children and adolescents. *J Am Acad Child Adolesc Psychiatry*. 1997;36(1):37–44.

figure if someone is still struggling with the idea of offering their child or young adult with a diagnosis ADHD medication.

CANNABIS IS HIGH ON THE LIST

Whenever I would stop smoking tobacco, cannabis would be the main reason I would start again. Giving up tobacco delivered a restless energy that I would have to push through by taking up swimming or some other activity overnight. I wrote about my ninth attempt at giving up in an article[41] that revealed I had done the Easy Way to Stop Smoking course three times, two hypnotherapy sessions, one reflexology course, and one acupuncture needle in the ear. On my tenth attempt, I decided that perhaps it wasn't the world that was out of kilter after all, it was me all along, and it prompted me to see the doctor to self-refer for an ADHD diagnosis the next day.

After my diagnosis, I was involved in a controlled trial of a cannabis-based Sativex inhaler to be used to calm ADHD symptoms. The six-week trial was double-blind, but I knew pretty early on that I was puffing on a placebo. The "active" group had better scores for cognitive ability and reduced hyperactivity than us placebos, who had to refrain from anything psychoactive during the trial. Although the pilot study included just thirty of us, the conclusion was far-reaching: "Adults with ADHD may represent a subgroup of individuals who experience a reduction of symptoms and no cognitive impairments following cannabinoid use".[42] This really was news, and explained in some part why others might give up using something like cannabis after their university days (the hangover and feeling too fuzzy at work the next day), while those with ADHD would wake the next morning and start the new day as fresh as picked lettuce.

---

[41] Mahony, E, *Can Barack Obama Kick his Nasty Habit?* 2009 <https://www.thetimes.co.uk/article/can-barack-obama-kick-his-nasty-habit-9fcbvnmbqq8> [accessed September 2018].

[42] Asherson, P, Cooper, R, 'Treatment of ADHD with cannabinoids : Abstract of the 25th European Congress of Psychiatry', *European Psychiatry*. Vol. 41, Supplement. (2017) pp. S55.

The law around cannabis has changed considerably since my university days, and in November 2018 it was legalised in the UK for medical use, so we are probably only a generation away from reducing the 8,000 people jailed since 2015 for cannabis-related offences. This costs the UK taxpayer £2.5 billion annually. Surely, it would be better to tax it? Some estimates suggest that it would raise £1 billion–3.5 billion annually if it was taxed. The UK's current prime minister Boris Johnson, and at least nine other present or former Conservative cabinet members, have admitted to using cannabis[43], so you could describe Generation X as "the people our parents warned us about". I hope that the future includes a model like Canada, where it has been legalised since 2019 for recreational use.

HOW TO UNDERSTAND THE EFFECTS OF CANNABIS ON ADHD

While the sale of medical marijuana strains might change, as it has in a number of US states, the science behind understanding how cannabis works on the brain is still relatively new. In the early 1990s, scientists discovered a cannabinoid receptor hardwired in the human brain, meaning that every human has an endocannabinoid system (ECS). The ECS is understood to contribute to self-regulation, keeping us level in anxious situations, helping with pain, and numerous other conditions from MS to epilepsy that need the mind and the body to work together to keep calm and carry on.

Without going into too much scientific detail, the psychoactive part of cannabis is called THC, which is what makes those who take it get high. In addition to THC, there are two other elements to the plant: CBN and CBD, which both have a calming and anti-anxiety effect. It's now understood that the endocannabinoid system within all of us is comprised of cannabinoid receptors, binding molecules for those receptors, and enzymes that synthesise and degrade the binding molecules.

[43] The Times, Friday 27 December 2019

When I volunteered for the trial organised by Kings College London[44], for the use of Sativex, the medical form of marijuana with THC and CBD in the form of a nose spray, the trial was looking only at those with an ADHD diagnosis. Little research had been done until this trial on cannabis use and ADHD, with most of the evidence to date being anecdotal. Sativex was authorised for use in the UK in 2010 for MS sufferers, but may also help ADHD sufferers who often turn to cannabis to alleviate symptoms. According to the trial research, many diagnosed adults prefer to manage their symptoms with cannabis rather than ADHD stimulant medication. However, many people with ADHD develop a dependency on cannabis, which also has links to schizophrenia and other mental health issues, which is another reason why safer forms of taking it need to be found. In 2016 the prevalence of ADHDers seeking treatment for Cannabis Use Disorder (CUD) was up to 46% of the total number that doctors encountered in a study in New York.[45]

PROFILE OF PHIL ANDERTON

Phil Anderton is author of The Tipping Points, a book that highlights the key points in an ADHDer's life when an intervention from a professional can make a radical difference to their life chances. Anderton served as a police officer for twenty-seven years, responsible for youth crime and mental health issues, and now works alongside ADDISS, the UK's ADHD information service, as their criminal justice advisor. In 2002 he was the Crime Concern Problem Solver of the Year as a result of his crime reduction successes in Lancashire.

[44] Cooper, R.E., Williams, E, Seegobin, S, Tye, C, Kuntsi, J, Asherson, P., Cannabinoids in attention-deficit/hyperactivity disorder: A randomised-controlled trial. *Eur Neuropsychopharmacol*.27(8), (2017), pp.795–808.

[45] Notzon, D.P., et al., 2016, 'ADHD Is Highly Prevalent in Patients Seeking Treatment for Cannabis Use Disorders.' Journal of attention disorders <https://www.ncbi.nlm.nih.gov/pmc/articles/PMC5568505/> [accessed September 2018]

Anderton's particular interest was in ADHD and crime, and the idea that "the criminal justice, legal, police system, and society in general at the moment appear to have a low awareness that there may well be a genetic or biological basis to some criminal activity."[46]

He looked at longitudinal studies of criminal behaviour in the US. People with ADHD were twice as likely to commit criminal offences, and compared to a control group who were arrested, they were committing three times as many offences. Included in those offences were drug-related crimes including possession, supplying, and stealing to provide for a habit. (In her book *ADHD in Adults* Susan Young, found that around 30% of the British prison population, two-thirds of all those in prison, had ADHD in childhood).[47]

Anderton looks at the figures for problematic drug use, and how that then turns to something more damaging for these young offenders. His work has been important in educating the health professionals, teachers, support and social workers, prison officers, and police to recognise the points in a young person's life, including something as simple as early and persistent smoking, where you might be able to support, rather than punish, a young person to turn away from criminal behaviour. He sweeps aside the moral notions around drug use to motivate ADHD users and help them find a better life. Some of the people profiled in the case studies in the book have gone on to make impressive life changes, including being accepted into Oxbridge universities after this kind of support, showing the transformative power of just understanding this condition.

---

46 Keley, G, *ADHD: recognition, reality and resolution* (Horsham: Learning Assessment Centre Press, 1999).

47 Braham, J, Young, S, *ADHD in Adults: A Psychological Guide to Practice* (Chichester: John Wiley & Sons Ltd., 2007). p. 119.

Now the managing director of an ADHD specialist healthcare provider, Phil Anderton set up ADHD 360 with a team of clinicians across the UK to treat those very people that he wrote about in his book. Treating alcohol and drug users, and young children who need help to avoid a potentially criminal life, means Anderton is now delivering the services he advocated for back at the start of the century.

CALL TO ACTION

Adults with ADHD should be wary around using cannabis to alleviate symptoms because dependency, psychosis, and currently a possible jail sentence could result (in the UK). However, governments need to renew the policies that are criminalising ordinary citizens by blocking them from accessing cannabis medicinally. If you or a loved one is a chronic cannabis user, might ADHD add to the picture of why they are?

PART 2
SURVIVE

CHAPTER 7
KNOW THYSELF

"We are all on a path, we are all making progress, and along the way we need to be ready to abandon our current view so we can be open to a new, better and deeper view, one which brings us closer to the truth; one which is more helpful for transforming our suffering and cultivating happiness."

Thich Nhat Han, *The Art of Living*

As I mentioned in the introduction, diagnosis is a double-edged sword. On the one hand, you have insight and knowledge into why some things occurred in your life. But, in my case, to be diagnosed so late, aged fifty-one, also brings with it regret, even grief, to look back at your life and think, 'If only I knew.' 'If only I knew … I might have had the benefit of medication and not flunked those exams at school/not got fired (again)/bust up that relationship for the hell of it/crashed that car/fallen out with that friend.' The list goes on.

Poor emotional control, outbursts of anger, risky behaviour, letting people down, and always being late, means that only a certain type of friend or partner can handle the ups and downs of a relationship or friendship with me. Sometimes, I think I created a drama just to pique my interest and stir things up a bit (that pesky dopamine fix).

More complicated than the simple, 'What I wish I knew at eighteen' line of thinking is the more subtle erosion of the times I believed fervently that I was in the right, but now realise that, actually, I was probably in the wrong all along. I have fought so many battles over the years, particularly with people in authority, convinced I was right – even arguing that getting a parking ticket while looking for change was an abuse of my human rights! I look back and think how many more worthy causes I could have fought for instead of getting into foolish fights with the Inland Revenue over late penalties, with all the passion of someone who was championing a Nelson Mandela cause.

Knowing that somehow the bundle of traits that make up ADHD – the restlessness, the impulsivity, and the distraction – don't lead to your house being orderly, your bank account being balanced, your three children being on track academically, or your freelance career being well managed, might have been useful to my sense of self and given me an awareness of my capabilities and limitations. Instead of insisting on doing what everyone else did, I could have just been kinder to myself about needing a bit more support to keep my house in order, and got on with the things I was good at. Often, being found wanting would lead to aggression and defensiveness, itself born out of frustration, and a level of drama that didn't help to keep a harmonious household when raising kids. All of that makes you look back on some of those days (if you can remember them) with regret and a grimace.

And so, with the diagnosis, which took a long time to seep in, came a creeping sense that it was probably me that was so often in the wrong, not him or her, and therefore now I employ a pre-emptive climb-down on arguments, whereas before I may have used a force-ten whirlwind of accusations. There is a part of me that actually likes confrontation, my protection was my aggression, and the worst part is that I was usually unaware that I was using it. I met a friend in a bar in London who has since qualified as a lawyer and reminded me how I pushed her chair back against a window at school and she smashed it, something I have absolutely no recollection of whatsoever. My children also remind me of occasions when I grabbed them by the scruff of the neck in anger because they had drifted into a shop when I was late to collect them, and still remember outbursts of anger over events that have not registered in my memory. Like the members of Alcoholics Anonymous who get to step 8 on their 12-step journey and vow to make amends to "all persons we have harmed", so an ADHD diagnosis comes with a giant apology letter to all those caught in the crossfire of unacceptable behaviour.

So today, if someone takes me to task over something that is an obvious ADHD trait, such as a forgotten meeting or a failure to set homework in my new role as a teacher, I check myself and assume first that I am in the wrong. What a difference from my former self, and the lengths I would go to in a bid to prove myself in the right. It is actually a relief, this letting go. I have let go of needing to be right, and learnt to be comfortable with the idea of being in the wrong.

After diagnosis, as well as having this newfound understanding that it was probably me who was in the wrong all along, when I brushed up against new problems, I then experienced a faltering sense of identity. Gone was the raging bull mentality, which could push on through most situations with the force of personality. Now there was a more hesitant drawing of breath. A quicker nod towards taking responsibility, and (I hope) to saying sorry. The diagnosis also came at a time of the milestone birthday of fifty, a time when questions about what you have achieved mixed with the fragility of existence, is always uppermost in your mind. For someone who has always used charm to explain away lost train tickets, or entry into sports/theatre previews, now, in middle age, I was expected to be responsible, and I couldn't always rely on a young person's winning smile.

I won't pretend that this period of rewriting history was a fast or easy one, over in a couple of weeks or months, and I emerged like a phoenix from the ashes – reborn as a better person. The guilt of being a newly diagnosed mother made me wince to remember how my mothering might have been (disorganised, inconsistent, distracted, explosive). However, as I dusted myself down, I ultimately felt fortunate to have kept myself and my family intact, and, most importantly, alive. Without getting out the small violins,

I eventually came round to what was important – not the little things, but the big things – letting them know they were loved.

SELF-JUSTIFICATION

I notice that people make up stories about their lives to help them make sense of it. As I mentioned earlier, when interviewing the most hardened of criminals, they would have a narrative to justify their actions. When something happens to someone, I believe they always learn to make sense of it by justifying it. Now I have my diagnosis, I wouldn't change place with *not* knowing I had it. I have changed as a result, but mainly in my understanding of myself.

I would say that as well as taking responsibility for my mistakes, I am also better able to go into situations knowing how they might pan out. Today my father talked about how perhaps the ADHDer is too busy being busy to mind, or notice, or get upset by the idea that they might be doing something wrong. After a lot of denial, my eighty-six-year-old father is finally admitting that he might be the source of our family ADHD, and he has certainly had a lifetime of being at war with my mother (amazingly, they are still married after fifty-plus years). Of course, he would never seek a diagnosis (or possibly even get one on the NHS at his age), but he is coming around to the idea that it explains a lot about his past life. As a young boy growing up in a large family, he was spared the pressure of higher education to leave for Royal Naval College at Dartmouth at sixteen, where he was given structure and discipline, which served him well. His ADHD didn't really show up until he left the Royal Navy. For a young girl, the impact can be different – lacking self-awareness and being firmly rooted in the now, instead of planning ahead, can have different consequences.

GIRLS AND ADHD

Sari Solden, who has been a practising psychotherapist for over thirty years, particularly working with women with ADHD, says: "The reason early identification of girls is so important is that years of being mislabelled, misunderstood or just plain missed can lead to serious long-term impacts on their self-esteem, relationships, achievement and emotions." And yet, how do you broach the subject of ADHD, with either the pupil or the parent, when neither really wants to hear it?

I see the undiagnosed ADHD children in my classes as a newly qualified secondary school teacher, but trying to raise the subject has done nothing but get me into trouble with the senior leadership team. Despite being open about my own ADHD in the four schools I have worked in to date, I have been put on "personal and professional conduct" just for talking to a teaching assistant about a pupil that she was supporting, and offering to speak to the parents about the child's uncontrollable ADHD. I have also been pulled up by a head of department for mentioning ADHD traits to a pupil, after a parent phoned to complain. I have even been taken into a room by a member of the senior leadership team to be hauled over the coals for "not being a medical expert", for a conversation that was referred to as an "incident" for the remainder of my training period in this particular school, again for raising the issue of ADHD to a fellow professional who reported me. It made me realise that in the current state of UK education, only parents can advocate for their children. Teachers, who are on the front line and see it daily, are not encouraged to help.

So, I have learnt to be quiet, shut up, and put up. Accept that on some level in the rural outreaches where I have so far had my teaching experience, at least, Victorian values prevail and schools prefer to label children as "naughty" and issue endless detentions, rather than challenge the root of the underlying behaviour. It then falls back on the parent to do the work to get their children the help they need, and if they are themselves resistant because of the stigma of their child being labelled, there is little that can be done.

STIGMA OF LABELS

Until the stigma of labels recede, it seems that everyone has to come to the issue when they are ready, and, in the meantime, all that can be done is to educate the parents, and the educators themselves, about the positive aspects of accepting this neurological difference. Few want to accept they have a learning disorder or mental health issue, or realise that by doing so they would then automatically be protected and offered *by law* all sorts of benefits to help them. The truth is that ADHD is still demonised, it is still a label with a stigma, so lack of diagnosis continues to prevail in this country, despite all the media headlines about the number of child diagnoses rocketing.

Back in the 1970s, mental health was rarely mentioned in the context of an English boarding school, especially one that was mainly focused on achievement. And yet my struggle to survive in a system so far removed from the comforts of home meant that I adopted a survivalist strategy, common with the rest of my boarding school generation. I knew how to duck, dive, and deceive to get myself out of trouble. This adaptability, plus the masses of sport offered up to boarding school children to keep them tired out and out of trouble, was to be my saviour. A reminder that there are many strengths to the ADHD arsenal of traits. Not least was how I channelled my energy into representing the school in many sports – netball, hockey, volleyball, rounders, athletics, and basketball, and how vital access to sports programmes are in schools.

This relationship between ADHD and exercise, or sport, is a well-documented one. And because I am keen to find a strengths-based approach to this disorder, it is perhaps a good moment to offer up the best poster boy we have when it comes to illustrating this point. Why Michael Phelps always makes it on to my list is because he has had all the typical ups and downs, bloops and blunders, of any ADHDer, but has triumphed to become not only the most decorated Olympian in history, but also someone who has given back in a big way to help others through his foundation. He is an extreme example, but he also represents the very best that can come out of channeling energy into something positive.

PROFILE OF MICHAEL PHELPS, US OLYMPIC SWIMMER

In April 2017, Michael Phelps made a video for the Child Mind Institute's annual public education campaign on mental health: "Speak up for Kids". In it, he talks about how he struggled with his ADHD as a child, and how a teacher had commented that "I would never amount to anything and I would never be successful." How very wrong they were. Phelps went on to win twenty-three gold medals, become the first American swimmer to compete in five Olympic games, and still currently holds the record for the most Olympic Golds in a single Olympics (eight golds in Beijing). He is also clearly someone that has put hyperfocus and hyperactivity to good use with the foundation that he set up later in life.

In his memoir *Beneath the Surface*, he remembers his childhood: "I simply couldn't sit still," he recounts, "it was difficult for me to focus on one thing at a time. When I was in sixth grade [Year Seven in the UK], Dr Wax diagnosed me with ADHD ... I started taking Ritalin three times a day." Phelps talks about the stigma of going to see the nurse in the middle of the school day to take his meds, or being hauled out of class if he forgot, and by seventh grade, he begged his mother to let him come off the medication. In Phelps' autobiography, he mentions how his mother (a middle-school head teacher) had him swimming from an early age to control his restlessness, and channel his "bouncing off the walls". He writes movingly about his mother, and the trials of being in school on and off Ritalin, and of the structure and support that his mother and a tough swimming coach gave him.

In 2008, he set up the Michael Phelps Foundation, with the IM Program (named after his signature stroke – the individual medley) to encourage children into the pool and to learn to swim safely. Difficult as it may be to believe, as a young boy Phelps had an initial fear of water, and it took a lot for him to learn to swim. In 2018, the programme celebrated its tenth anniversary by launching across seven countries and six continents to help 22,000 people to learn to swim over the decade. Phelps describes helping others who are struggling as being something that has been "way more powerful" for him than winning medals. By focusing on the importance of teaching children water safety, the IM Program aims to reduce half a million annual deaths by drowning, and to help children get over a fear of water. It added mental health to its teaching curriculum with the IM Healthy Program in 2018, teaching children basic emotional skills as well.

The emphasis on mental health comes from Phelps' own life where he has stated publicly his challenges with depression and suicidal thoughts. He has also had a number of very public brushes with the law for driving under the influence of alcohol, speeding, and, in 2009, he was photographed at a party using a "cannabis bong", an image that went viral, causing him to be banned by USA Swimming for six months. Somehow, Michael managed to bounce back and speak honestly about his difficulties. Talking about his ADHD to *People* magazine in 2017 he said: "It's something that I'm thankful happened, and I'm thankful that I am how I am."

Today, he says he has learnt to deal with the condition through talking about it and having therapy. "I think the biggest thing for me was once I found that it was okay to talk to someone and seek help, I think that's something that has changed my life forever," he says. "Now I'm able to live life to its fullest."

CALL TO ACTION

If you know your triggers, how you tick, and how you might need to be extra cautious in the parts of your life, or the life of someone with ADHD, where impulsivity, restlessness, and distraction show up, then you can adapt your behaviour accordingly. As a person with ADHD you can learn to control the impulses instead of being controlled by them, or if you are someone who lives with ADHD in their life, you can begin not to take it personally. This is the beginning of forgiveness for some of the mistakes that have been made, whether by you or to you, because it may have been ADHD at the root cause. Forgiveness or self-forgiveness is obviously very healing, because it allows another level of compassion to yourself or to someone else. Acceptance of ADHD in a life can bring grief, but ultimately it is the beginning of a deeper and more meaningful relationship with others and the world.

CHAPTER 8
EDUCATION

"For many, school can be an incubator for success. For ADHDers, it is often a breeding ground for failure."
Kevin Roberts, author of *Movers, Dreamers and Risk-Takers*

There is no doubt that the hormone surge in puberty and during the teenage years has a profound effect on ADHD. Although there is relatively little research around girls, and what has been done has mostly been corralled by Professor Hinshaw (see page 100), the hormone surge for boys is well documented. It is often given as the reason why so many more boys than girls are likely to be diagnosed, because a testosterone surge is associated with risky activity and acting out, which is more likely to be picked up in a school environment.

Conversely, a surge in oestrogen for girls has more of an internalising effect, affecting mood and emotional stability, and if not recognized, can lead to self-harming or anxiety and depression. This is still a new area of research, although some limited studies have already shown how ADHD symptoms fluctuate in girls over the menstrual cycle, suggesting there is a definite link between oestrogen (a stimulant) and ADHD. Also, what studies there are tend to follow young girls who have already been diagnosed, and therefore may already be on medication, making it even harder to see the true picture of what impact hormones may have on the undiagnosed and untreated adolescent.

There are four significant hormonal periods across a woman's lifespan: puberty, pregnancy, peri-menopause, and post-menopause, and they are all significant in my personal experience of having ADHD and being untreated. In teenage times, it is that surge in hormones that comes into play, and when I reflected upon my school years as part of my diagnosis – and was asked to bring in my school reports – it was there in black and white, some thirty-odd years later.

BRIGHT BUT BADLY BEHAVED

Despite being a scholarship girl, I became a rebel out of the classroom at boarding school. For offences deemed big enough for proper punishment, my British boarding school enforced 'gatings'. Gatings meant: *no make-up, no jewellery, tan-coloured tights, and no outings during the break periods.* Like a prisoner with an electronic tag, you had to stay inside and report to the Head of House every break time. At my prep school, my Head of House was a certain Ghislaine Maxwell, daughter of the late tycoon and newspaper proprietor Robert Maxwell, who has recently been accused of procuring under-age girls for sex-trafficking for the disgraced billionaire, the late Jeffery Epstein. Even back then at school, she was a rather fearsome figure, and I was gated thirteen times throughout my school career, so enjoyed a number of run-ins with her. Most pupils were suspended after two gatings, then expelled after suspension, so somehow I managed to cling on to my place at school, probably by contributing to the school through team sports.

My rebelliousness was a desire to take risks, just for the sake of it. In my reports excavated for the ADHD diagnosis, it is there in black and white in a letter, dated 3rd March 1979, from my housemaster – a figure who stood *in loco parentis* when our parents barely saw us from one half of term to the next. He wrote to my father: *You may remember that on the Christmas report we indicated that Emma's initial behaviour at the start of the school year was very unsatisfactory, but that after the half-term she appeared to settle down, thus prompting us to make some very encouraging remarks about the future.*

Sadly, this was optimistic, as she has a poor record this term in the house of disobedience and disruptive behaviour, with a second school gating for smoking.

This was particularly frustrating for us, as barely forty-eight hours earlier I had given her a friendly "fatherly" talk on the lines that she was halfway through her fifth year, with exams ahead and only a few months from the sixth form and sixth-form responsibilities (such as possible prefect status). She had been banned for some weeks from the fifth form prep rooms on the top floor, which I had specially organised for this examination group, because of her behaviour, and this I proposed to end with the promise of a responsible attitude – after the obvious warning of the first school gating for a drink offence two weeks ago. This is the first time that we have resorted to a school gating, but we hope that the treatment will have the desired effect.

I was fifteen and it didn't. Nor did I ever make a prefect, the only Oxbridge candidate at the school who wasn't one. My point is that the ADHD is there in the school reports and letters home. In those days, my behaviour might have been seen as just teenage high jinks – except that it has an additional edge to it. Although others may have been involved, I tended to be the one caught, the first to suggest to ride in the boot of the bus, to climb the roof of the indoor tennis court. There was little forethought, the impulsivity is there writ large.

SCHOOL REPORTS

Not only did I not like being told what to do, I also didn't like to tell others what to do. I quickly became labelled as "naughty". As a teacher now, I've noticed this is still the staffroom-preferred shorthand for many undiagnosed ADHD children, and I wince as I listen to the teaching assistants trade children's behaviour like Top Trumps: who is the "naughtiest" that they are assigned to. I was in trouble often, and as that reputation began to cement itself, it was all too easy to play to the gallery. The ADHD expert Dr Hallowell might call my misdemeanours "high stim" (as in high stimulation) activity, such as making daring raids on the house larder in the dead of night, when the rest of the house was tucked up in bed. We used to court the local boys in our Somerset village and sneak out of the house in our nighties to get in the car with them, to go and climb the Glastonbury Tor. It is slightly hair-raising to think this went on, and when I revisited my school I saw that CCTV has now put paid to such activity.

High jinks also veered into criminal activity, as I began shoplifting with my new best friend, who would encourage me to wear a large coat and open the bags when she lifted the products from the local high street. Perhaps unsurprisingly, I recently learnt that "The most common form of antisocial activity for adults with ADHD was shoplifting (53%)."[48]

Such behaviour also showed up in the academic area, where I was expected to perform better than those not in scholarship sets, but was also busy offering up my test papers to others during exams through a "coughing and dropping" routine. In the peculiarly un-PC language of forty years ago, my hormonal behaviour was showing in reports where I have put in bold what the psychiatrist picked up on. In maths: *For much of the term, Emma has been full of good intentions and goodwill but* ***totally disorganized.*** Or music, where Mr Keating described me as a *rather* ***"scatty"*** *but lively member of the group*. My housemistress, Mrs Lobb, wrote: *Emma is slowly improving.* ***She still leaves her prep books all over the house.*** *But she has managed to gain control over her clothes. She is a kind, cheerful girl and does her house duties willingly.*

The following year Mr Gilchrist, my maths teacher became my housemaster, and was now clearly losing patience: *She is the weak member of the set and I sometimes* ***wonder how much of her mind is on the job at hand,*** *as her comments and* ***questions are sometimes totally irrelevant.*** *However, somehow she manages to obtain a fair proportion of right answers – possibly found through intuition.* As for the house, Mr Gilchrist added: *She* ***is untidy and scatter-brained,*** *but she gets her peers to work well with her and has been quite an effective monitor –* ***when she remembers!*** *She has a delightful personality and is popular with both peers and adults, but sometimes* ***her absent-mindedness is exasperating.***

---

[48] Barkley, R.A., Murphy, K.R., and Fischer M. *ADHD in Adults: what the science says* (New York: Guildford Press, 2011).

NON-MEDICATION VS MEDICATION

By the time I got to my mid-teens, I had to put away my desire to be recognised as one of the school champions. Yesterday, I was at a prize-giving where my ADHD son's school table groaned with the prizes to be awarded, many of which had built up over the 500 years his grammar school had been in existence. There was a sense that the school wanted to recognise as many pupils as possible; each subject had a prize, sometimes two: one for effort and one for achievement, as well as prizes for courage, outstanding academic achievement in that year, sports, overall and individual. As I sat there clapping for over an hour, I couldn't help remembering my own school experience; it doesn't matter what age you are – prize-giving does that. The truth was, by the time I got to the sixth form, I was the opposite of prize-winning material. I'd had my moments in the school teams, including being captain of the A Team for hockey, but then I was asked to step down the following term after I had forgotten to bring the team shirts in a match against Cheltenham Ladies' College, so we had had to wear their Second Team spare shirts. The school hockey mistress never forgave me for humiliating the school.

My defence was to appear as if I didn't give a damn. By then, I had created a persona of a fully paid-up rebel, and prizes weren't cool. My persona was also a way of deflecting from some innate lack of trust in myself; I knew that I would falter and could not perform on demand.

Back at my ADHD son Michael's prize-giving, in the car on the way home, as he sat with a certificate for the Spanish prize for the second year in a row, I discussed how he felt about taking medication. I asked him if it was important to him to get that recognition through his school report and this sort of prize. We talked about his first year at secondary school when he got suspended and how his medication had helped him. I made the connection between how the experience of succeeding at something early on can be crucial for self-esteem, rather than building up a persona that is at best entertaining, at worst self-destructive.

And yet, until my diagnosis, I almost felt more comfortable with disapproval than with approbation. I'd developed coping skills, and used my charm and humour to survive situations, but it was a front. Because of course I cared. Everyone does. But caring invites vulnerability, and I was working hard at covering up that side wherever possible.

UNDERPERFORMANCE

As I turned eighteen and prepared for my A-level exams in my final year at school, I adopted a new attitude – and just like that, the rebellion was replaced with obsession. I wanted to do well academically, even if I already had a bad reputation behaviourally, to prove that I was worthy of that academic scholarship with which I was ushered into the school.

With my usual lack of balance, as I mentioned earlier, I was getting up at 6 am, revising all day, sometimes with barely a break, until 1 am. Sixth formers in their final year were given their own room, so nobody would check when I would finally turn off my light and go to bed. And if you were working, that was good wasn't it? I was taking A-levels in Russian and French, and had started Russian A-level from scratch to take the GCSE in a year in the Lower Sixth, and then the A-level the following year. It was ambitious to do a language to A-level in a year, but I had a kind, sensitive teacher in Mr Adams, who genuinely looked forward to sharing his enthusiasm for the language and literature.

As a teenager, I was a personality riddle to myself, and I could end up with mini internal meltdowns when asked to, say, read in class. I don't consider this to be related to my ADHD, but suddenly my cheeks would start burning, my throat would become completely dry, and I literally could not speak. All I could hear was the sound of my heart thumping – 'like trainers in the tumble dryer', as David Foster Wallace describes it in his book *Infinite Jest* – and my urge would be to flee the room if asked to read something.

So bad was this sort of performance anxiety that I chose to read French and Russian as modern languages for A-level, despite being in love with English literature. I seemed to feel more at home communicating in a different language, or inhabiting a foreign skin.

The state of hyperfocus (see page 33) I went into around my A-levels was unhealthy and resulted in a completely overblown revision pattern, which probably lacked real organisation. I believed that hard work led to good results – that was the school motto, wasn't it? "*Molire molendo* – ground by grinding" – so when I opened my A-level results after predictions of Bs to find I had three Ds, I nosedived. It wasn't through lack of effort; something else had happened. Somehow that promise had faltered, and I had known for sure that there were occasions when I couldn't be trusted. I didn't know why, but I knew it was true. It was an academic slap in the face. I spent weeks sulking in my room, unsure what to do next. However, the predictions had already got me offers in good universities, and my parents agreed to let me to return to do that extra term for Oxbridge despite all hopes being dashed by my grades. I was lucky. I had all the support a middle-class education could throw at a situation. How many other ADHD teenagers can count on such good fortune?

PROFILE OF DR STEPHEN HINSHAW

Dr Stephen Hinshaw is a professor at the Department of Psychology at the University of California, Berkeley, and Vice Chair for Child and Adolescent Psychology. Recently his book *Another Kind of Madness: A Journey Through the Stigma and Hope of Mental Illness* won Best Book in the American Book Fest 2018 (autobiography/memoir). Professor Hinshaw is one of a few researchers who has been undertaking longitudinal studies of the effects of hormones on girls with ADHD, studying them for more than sixteen years. Here he comments:

We found that girls with ADHD in their early teens have more academic problems, more aggressive behaviour, some earlier signs of substance-related problems, and higher rates of depression than girls who don't have the condition.[49]

As girls with ADHD mature into adolescence, and beyond, on average they don't show as many visible symptoms of the condition, especially the most noticeable form – hyperactive behaviour. But we can't get fooled into thinking things are fine. Delinquent and depressed behaviours, risk for substance abuse, symptoms of eating disorders, extremely high risk for self-harm (both non-suicidal self-injury and actual suicide attempts), a high need for services, difficulties with peers – these problems hit girls with ADHD harder than they do for the comparison group without the condition.

Even more, by their early to mid-20s, the girls who had been carefully diagnosed with ADHD in childhood showed major issues with post-secondary education; continued risk for self-injury, and a markedly higher rate of unplanned pregnancies (45% vs. 10% in the matched comparison sample). On the other hand, unlike many boys with ADHD, the girls in this sample did not show elevated risk for substance abuse in their twenties.

[49] Owens, E.B., Zalecki, C, Gillette, P, Hinshaw, S.P., Girls with childhood ADHD as adults: Cross-domain outcomes by diagnostic status. Journal of Consulting and Clinical Psychology, (2017), 723–736.

CALL TO ACTION

What were you or your loved one like as a teenager? Can you find some old school reports and look for evidence beyond the family script that might have a different take on your adolescence? Teenage diaries may be one part of the puzzle, but it is the observations of those in authority that offer proper evidence of acting out in a harmful way. As women in particular are often disbelieved, or even refused diagnosis on the basis of their better-than-average grades at school[50], researching your own struggles with restlessness, impulsivity, and distraction in these years might bolster your confidence in seeking a diagnosis.

---

50 Ellison, K, '*How women and girls with ADHD are given short shrift with treatment, other forms of help*', 2020 https://www.washingtonpost.com/health/how-women-and-girls-with-adhd-are-given-short-shrift-with-treatment-other-forms-of-help/2020/05/15/ a7971486-8596-11ea-878a-86477a724bdb_story.html [accessed May 2020].

CHAPTER 9
ENTREPRENEURSHIP

"If someone told me you could be normal or you could continue to have your ADHD, I would take ADHD."
David Neeleman, founder of JetBlue Airways

The science behind ADHD and entrepreneurship suggests that both hyperactivity and the multifaceted trait of impulsivity[51] can be beneficial to being an entrepreneur. Also, those with ADHD symptoms may be empowered to craft their own jobs to fit their square-peg-in-a-round-hole way of operating, so they aren't beholden to fitting in with a particular work culture. A recent paper by the Yale School of Public Health found that children with ADHD are 10–14% less likely to be employed as adults, and ADHD employees earn as much as 33% less[52] income than neurotypicals.

If these are the negative aspects for the ADHDer employee, who can become easily bored with routine and keen to seek novelty or take risks, then they can also be translated into positives when setting up in business. If you add hyperfocus (see page 33) into the mix, because the person with ADHD is doing something creative that they are interested in, then the passion and persistence needed to push the idea through is there as well.

---

51 Wiklund, J, Patzelt, H, Dimov, D, Entrepreneurship and psychological disorders: How ADHD can be productively harnessed. *Journal of Business Venturing Insights*, 6(14), 2016, DOI: 10.1016/j.jbvi.2016.07.001

52 Weissmann, J, *Study: Children With ADHD Earn Less, Work Less Later In Life*, 2013 <https://www.theatlantic.com/business/archive/2013/01/study-children-with-adhd-earn- less-work-less-later-in-life/267220/> [accessed October 2018].

Setting up in business is not about waiting around for the phone to ring, so the speed aspect and instant feedback are added grist to the mill, as is thriving in a high stakes and pressured environment.

Dr Dale Archer adds in his book *The ADHD Advantage*[53] the trait of "multi-tasking" to the list, because owners of start-up companies often have to juggle many tasks from sales to purchasing, because they can't always afford the staff to begin with. This varied diet of different jobs wrapped into one purpose suits the ADHDer's personality well, due to their ability to spring from one task to the next without losing sight of the goal. Suddenly that distractibility translates into plate spinning, all that rushing around keeping those plates going is a bonus quality.

As Dr Archer also mentions, where those of us with ADHD may fail as entrepreneurs is in outsourcing to others important routine tasks such as book-keeping, doing taxes, and managing personnel, because otherwise they can get neglected. This was definitely my mistake when I had my own company for five years and we came to sell the student magazine I set up after university – in fact, we didn't even know we were in such debt until we totted up the figures for a buyer.

LAUNCHING *RASP* MAGAZINE

Dr Dale Archer reports that people with ADHD are three times more likely to set up in business[54], and I was no exception to the statistical rule. In 1990, after a year of a dead-end publishing job in Cricklewood, North London, followed by a short stint on the *Sunday Express* newspaper on Fleet Street, before it moved to new offices – I set up my own magazine, *RASP*, on jobs and careers for graduates. It was to be written by graduates, newly in the jobs themselves, to give undergraduates a taste of what was to come. I got the idea

[53] Archer, D, *The ADHD Advantage: what you thought was a diagnosis may be your greatest strength*, (New York: Penguin Random House 2015).

[54] Archer, D, *ADHD –the entrepreneur's superpower, 2014 <https://www.forbes.com/sites/dalearcher/2014/05/14/adhd-the-entrepreneurs-superpower/>* [accessed October 2019].

after seeing so many of my friends being clueless as they left university, with few of them knowing what they wanted to do career-wise. Those who did go for university careers advice were given the latest psychometric testing, and all seemed to fit the correct profile for 'landscape gardeners'. The risible careers advisory service at university showed the disconnect between education and real life – they needed to get away from their dusty shelves and find out what was really going on for those newly ejected graduates. This was before the internet, so first-hand information was hard to find – and the "milk round" only applied to a handful of possible corporate types – so we thought a magazine addressing this transition would be a good idea.

Big companies who wanted to recruit the "cream" of the milk round were to pay for the magazine in recruitment advertising. I had written for the university newspaper while at Exeter University, and produced a one-off satirical magazine *Comic Cuts* after final exams, so I had some experience in putting together a title. I recruited a business partner in Guy Ogilvy, who had left the university before me, and was living in a squat in Fulham with some members of his rock band. We felt confident that the magazine would appeal to fellow slackers like ourselves. We launched in a blaze of a new decade of optimism, just as the Berlin Wall came down in 1990. We rejected offers from investors after meeting a few other publishers, and decided to publish on our own because we wanted editorial independence.

As the recession bit, we also expanded to include an arts and music section, and while the magazine went down well in all the university newspaper offices across the country, where it was distributed as a supplement, Guy and I never successfully balanced the books. Our accountant ran off, having taken with him some clients' money, and it fell to me to do the company and VAT returns. Occasionally, we used to hide behind the filing cabinets when the Customs & Excise bailiffs came around, and we kept the whole thing going on a shoestring. Doing it our way meant preselling the first issue with £20,000 worth of advertising, and then juggling the printers and repro houses and distribution via Royal Mail, as well paying ourselves a pittance and putting an additional advertising salesperson on commission only.

Despite the lack of cash flow, Guy set up a popular "Battle of the Bands" competition for upcoming wannabe bands at universities nationwide, sponsored by Rebel Yell Whiskey. We landed many firsts, including the first interview with Oasis, when Guy saw Liam Gallagher perform in Manchester, and the first explanation of the potential of something then described as "the world wide web", and some of the more innovative content was sponsored by brands such as British Telecom, and the *Guardian*.

HYPERFOCUS IN BUSINESS

These were the entrepreneurial days of Prime Minister Margaret Thatcher, when it felt like any woman could wear shoulder pads and make a business happen, and it all felt within our reach. My job was to sell advertising space *and* edit the magazine – not a role usually straddled in the commercial world. If I had tried to keep a "balance" at university to stop me overworking, as I had done around my A-levels, I failed once again at this when I became stuck into my own company.

Hyperfocus (see page 33) sucked me in, the project consumed me, and whole weekends would be lost in company forms, VAT returns, accounts, commissioning, and chasing copy. I was incapable of not staying late at the office – when the phones went silent, and I felt I could finally get all my work done. I lost weight as I neglected myself with the stress of juggling too many roles. After the first year I became better at managing everything, although I would often experience migraines around the time of "putting the magazine to bed".

However, for all the downsides, I would have definitely added to a study that showed a significant positive link between ADHD diagnosis and "venturing/entrepreneurial action". In particular, having ADHD increases the odds of venturing by almost 100%. The results indicate that university-enrolled adults with ADHD are *almost two times more likely* to initiate entrepreneurial action than those without ADHD".[55]

IMPULSIVITY AND DECISION-MAKING

RASP was as much a lifestyle as work, offering anyone who wanted a job to have a go "space hustling", and anyone who could write a commission. We soon added gigs, theatre, and film to our pages – with random advertizers brought in by our brightest star Lucy Barker, who introduced me to her brother Adam, now my husband. However, if Guy had rock glamour with his long curly hair, and I had a dogged determination, neither of us knew the first thing about business. We were clearly winging it, and even the title was our own home-grown slang for to "talk on and on". We told advertizers it stood for "Real Answers to Student Prospects" and added the tagline: "Life after Graduation".

I believed then and still do, that anybody can write if they have a story to tell. New graduate accountants wrote the accountancy pieces, and the graduate lawyers wrote the law articles – nobody was a professional writer. Contributors were encouraged to be brutally honest, to tell it like it is, and were paid £50 per piece. Their copy would be whipped into shape by our eagle-eyed sub-editor Kate Chapple, herself moonlighting from a full-time position at *Country Life* magazine. We all spent a lot of time dreaming up what creative headlines we could get away with, without offending our advertisers, and next to each piece was a "How To Do the Job" guide, whom to write to, telephone numbers, which companies were recruiting.

Throughout the country, 40,000 copies of the magazine were slipped into student newspapers like a glossy Sunday supplement, and soon advertisers from beyond the careers market came on board, including film distributors. Our motto was "seriousness of purpose, frivolity of approach", and some issues were banned on

---

55 Lerner, D.A., Verheul, I, Thurik, R, Entrepreneurship and attention deficit/ hyperactivity disorder: a large-scale study involving the clinical condition of ADHD. *Small Bus Econ*, 53, (2019), pp.381–392.

student campuses because we insisted every issue had a real-life story of drugs. One front cover had "Magic Mushrooms: dangerous or just unpredictable?" and a number of universities decided that this was too much to include in their campus newspaper. Another university decided to have a debate over its distribution and freedom of speech. We lost a few advertisers along the way.

We pitched everyone and were terrier-like in our determination to make the magazine work, forgoing any useful income to keep the money in the company. I was taking home only £25 a week and living for free in my then boyfriend's flat, while Guy took only a small rise on that to keep his end of the squat up. It was easier to keep warm at the office than at home, so we rarely missed a day's work.

When I was headhunted to work at another magazine publisher, and looked to edit *RASP* in my time off, I saw for the first time how a proper small business was run – with bosses who went home at the end of the day, and people who were not completely consumed by their work. Reluctantly, Guy and I decided to sell the title. We'd had five fantastic years of fun, and sold it to TNT Publishing for £40,000. When we totted up our debts, they were almost exactly £40,000. We had emerged, without debt, but also without a penny.

Guy was also headhunted but decided to forgo his potentially lucrative career in publishing to go and live in a cave in the mountains of Central North Mexico for eighteen months, as a hermit. There he became interested in esotericism and alchemy, and has written several books under a pseudonym, which have been translated into more than twenty languages and have sold over 750,000 copies. He now lives near Glastonbury with his wife and five children, and still plays in a rock band.

But Lucy, who had cut her teeth on the magazine, was to be the most successful entrepreneur to come out of it. She would leave RASP to set up her own financially profitable company in Harrogate in Yorkshire. At its height, before her diagnosis with breast cancer, her company Barker Brooks media was employing fifty people and turning over millions of pounds. She set up dozens of contract titles, including the Apprenticeship guide which became the basis for the UK government's website, and the Yorkshire Lawyer's awards, which still run today. Every title she published had an event tacked on to it, a further excuse for a party, and she was shortlisted for *Veuve Cliquot Business Woman of the Year*. When she died in 2016, it was her obituary for the Times that they chose to be the face of their Christmas round-up of business people who had passed away that year, smiling back at the reader in front of framed magazine covers. A true RASPer, she embodied the spirit of bluff and chutzpah, seriousness of intent and frivolity of approach.

I kept the company for another year, and continued publishing other corporate customer magazines on my own. Then came an opportunity to work at *The Times* newspaper, and I found myself drawn back into newspaper journalism, but this time with the confidence of having run my own magazine company successfully (if not particularly profitably). It would be many years later, in 2016, when some academic research would investigate that positive connection between entrepreneurial activity and ADHD: *Thousands if not tens of thousands of academic papers have documented the negative implications of having ADHD and there seem to be many. Very few papers have examined or found support for any positive effects of the disorder but some anecdotal evidence suggests that ADHD could have positive implications in entrepreneurship.*[56] This multiple case study of fourteen entrepreneurs showed how the traits of impulsivity, with its decision-making and risk-taking based on "gut reaction" helped drive entrepreneurial success, with hyperfocus having both positive and negative consequences.

As the founder of Kinko's, a copying service now owned by FedEx and worth $2.4 billion says: "My biggest advantage is that I don't get bogged down by the details, because of my ADHD. I hire capable people to handle that."[57]

---

[56] Wiklund, J, Patzelt, H, Dimov, D, Entrepreneurship and psychological disorders: How ADHD can be productively harnessed. *Journal of Business Venturing Insights*, 6(14), 2016, DOI: 10.1016/j.jbvi.2016.07.001

[57] Gilman, L, *How to Succeed in Business with ADHD*, 2018. <https:// www.additudemag.com/adhd-entrepreneur-stories-jetblue-kinkos-jupitermedia/> [accessed December 2018].

TEN BEST AND WORST JOBS FOR AN ADHDER

With a nod to *ADDitude* magazine[58], who are often compiling these sort of lists, I present my own personal list of what to do and not to do on the job front. Pinch of salt at the ready.

Five of the worst:

1) **Corporate executive:** Unless you are working for a corporation bent on saving the planet, rather than making money for itself, stay clear of the corporate world. I have tried this and can report back that it was a disaster. The strict pecking order, the boring endless meetings (looking up from my computer and seeing an empty room because everyone was stuffed in a glass office where I was supposed to be), the self-importance of the senior executives, and the greasiness of that pole which others stand on your head to climb is the antithesis of the ADHD brain. I know I was fired, so I am obviously not bitter.
2) **Accountant:** The pain of filling in tiny boxes and then adding it all up, and then adding it all up again when you have just got distracted by a Milky Way chocolate bar on someone else's desk, would make this my official worst job in the world. I'd probably be in prison if accountants didn't exist, so they deserve their healthy monthly wages.
3) **Personal Assistant:** I was a personal assistant to the European Editor at *Fortune* magazine for a while, and never managed to learn how to put through a single call for him, because I couldn't operate the complicated phone system. Whenever anyone showed me, my mind just wandered off. Organising someone else's life was

58 https://www.additudemag.com/

also not a natural talent, and while we got on well, my boss waved a bit too cheerily when he saw me off to set up my own business.

4) **Events Planner:** Because all ADHDers are firmly stuck in the now, the idea of being able to plan in meticulous detail an event in the future seems a horrible fit. While I love to attend a party, I couldn't even plan activities in the holidays for the kids, let alone build a career out of doing it. This would be torture for me.
5) **Lawyer:** Just thinking of all those years of exams, and the need to be really devilish with the detail as all around you rely on your studied response, makes me shiver. My husband is a lawyer, albeit in a creative industry, and I marvel at how much effort and thought he can put into a contract for me, which I then have to force myself to read.

Five of the best:

1) **Teacher:** It seems unlikely in some ways, all that marking and workload, but if you are teaching a subject you love, then even lesson-planning is fascinating. The performance aspect of being at the front of the class keeps you on your toes, and all that interaction with pupils is never ever dull (if it is for you, then it definitely is for them, too). ADHDers are also helped by timetables and constant reminders from the bells.
2) **Armed forces:** As with teaching, structure actually supports an ADHDer, and the physical and social aspects of being in the military ensures that someone with ADHD will thrive on the connection to his group and higher purpose. My (ADHD) father was in the Royal Navy and loved it; the hardest part for him was finding an occupation that matched its excitement when it was time to leave.
3) **Food industry:** Being a chef, a sous-chef, even a kitchen porter – all these jobs require performance in a pressured environment, where there is plenty of camaraderie, lots

to do, and a creative element if you work to chef status. Michelin star chef Heston Blumenthal[59] says his ADHD helps him to think outside of the box, and he would not swop it for anything.

4) **Journalism:** As already outlined, the pressure of deadlines, the novelty of the new story, the performance element in TV journalism, all conspire to make journalism a great fit for ADHD traits. There are sub-editors waiting in the wings to correct mistakes, and the buzz from being part of a team working towards a common goal makes this a good collaborative choice.
5) **Entrepreneur:** There are now studies[60] that focus on the positives of ADHD in business, particularly the energy that allows the neuroatypical ADHDer to work longer hours, hyperfocus, and use impulsivity and risk-taking can be a bonus as a business expands. As long as the unenjoyable jobs are outsourced, working for yourself is a great idea.

---

59 Bloom, A, *Heston Blumenthal: 'I have ADHD. But I wouldn't change it for the world*, 2016 <https://www.tes.com/news/heston-blumenthal-i-have-adhd-i-wouldnt-change-it- world> [accessed October 2018].

60 Wiklund, J, Patzelt, H, Dimov, D, 'Entrepreneurship and psychological disorders: How ADHD can be productively harnessed', *Journal of Business Venturing Insights*, 6, (2016), pp.14–20.

PROFILE OF RORY BREMNER, COMEDIAN AND IMPRESSIONIST

Rory Bremner says: *I didn't realise I had ADHD until very recently, when a relative was diagnosed with the condition, and it dawned on me that we shared many of the symptoms such as impetuosity, distractibility, forgetfulness, and disorganisation.*

It's been a blessing for my career in many ways – for example, it means I am able to spot analogies and to think laterally in a comedic sense – however, it's no laughing matter for many children and adults living with the condition who simply don't have the professional help needed to learn how best to deal with their symptoms.

It's estimated that one in twenty have the condition – roughly half a million schoolchildren in the UK, which means, on average, one child in every class is often seen as restless, fidgety, distracted, or even disruptive. Yet, with the right diagnosis, approach, and understanding these youngsters are often the most creative and rewarding of all students.

Once seen as a behavioural – even a moral – problem, the science is now catching up with us, and it's recognised as a neuro-developmental "disorder". ADHD is a condition whose time has come, and it's crucial that we do all we can to understand it, recognise its effects, and support people living with it. The [newly established UK support group] ADHD Foundation is at the forefront in a breakthrough of understanding this condition, so now is an exciting time to really make some differences for children and families living with it.

CALL TO ACTION

Knowing that people with ADHD make good entrepreneurs, if they have the right support behind them, might it encourage you or someone you know to make the leap into a business? As well as being a good way to combine the interest, energy, and creativity of ADHD, it can also impress future employers, even if it does not work out in the long term. So, if you have yet to find an area of work that suits your mindset, and can start small to reduce financial risk, is setting up on your own a possibility? Would knowing you have ADHD, or a friend who has it, give you that extra push to try out on your own? Or even better, rope in someone with a steady hand on the tiller to do all the boring but important stuff, and thereby put profit before fun.

CHAPTER 10
JOBS AND CAREERS

"Many people with ADHD find careers or lifestyles where it's an asset rather than a handicap."
Rory Bremner, comedian and impressionist

When the NHS psychiatrist interviewed me to diagnoze my ADHD, one of the few moments he broke off from his rapid-fire questioning was when he looked up and asked how I had managed to sustain a journalism career. I told him that journalists have to write everything down (you have to in case you are ever sued), so you don't need to remember that much. Everything was there in my reporter's pad. All I had to do was try not to lose it. Also, the most equipment you need for being a journalist is a pen, and you can usually borrow one of those.

SITUATIONAL VARIABILITY

There is some research that says to manage ADHD successfully, one has to find the right job – it's called "Situational Variability". Thomas E Brown, the author of *Outside the Box: Rethinking ADHD in Children and Adults*, states: *… all individuals with ADHD seem to have some specific domains of activity in which they have no difficulty in performing these various functions that are, for them, so impaired in virtually every other area of life. Often ADHD patients describe this as simply a function of the level of their personal interest in the specific activity. This situational variability of the symptoms can be viewed as symptoms of the evidence that the impairments of the brain involved in ADHD are not* *with these fundamental cognitive functions themselves, but with the central management networks that turn them on and off.* [61]

Again, this suggests that ADHD is not so much a problem of attention as regulation. So, if you find the right job, or working environment in a position that you love, then the ADHD will not be as noticeable. As well as setting up in business, journalism for me was just that; it was exciting, it had time deadlines, and every story was new.

Journalism – whether radio, TV, print, magazines or online – is a pretty good profession for someone with ADHD. It's what Dr Hallowell would call high in "Vitamin C", or Vitamin Connect – you have to connect with people. It is also high stimulation, and the deadlines make you get out of bed to get the work done. Most importantly, there is novelty, because you are always working on a new story, and being "first with the news" is prized above all else. Finally, there is enough creativity in the writing or presenting, if words or performance are your thing, to keep you enjoying the challenge.

There is also something about journalism that you can't really train for, and that suits the restless, impulsive, distracted ADHD brain – it's the whiff of a good story, like a dog running off on the trail of a good scent. When I was starting out on the *Sunday Express* as a news reporter in 1987, I didn't really understand what this was – but I knew if I hung around people that did know long enough, I might pick it up. On the Saturday news pages of the *Sunday Express*, it wasn't up to us "cub reporters" to find the stories – the older editors wandered over to give us one to hunt down.

The badly dressed news editors would shuffle over to where we sat in front of giant heavy typewriters, capable of amputating a foot if they fell off a desk, hand us a bit of paper and say, 'I think this might be worth looking into.' Usually that was as much of a lead as the editors would give you, and if you didn't know what you were looking for, as I didn't in those early days, it was terrifying. You then had to persuade someone who knew what

---

61 Brown, T.E., *ADHD Comorbidities: Handbook for ADHD Complications in Children and Adults* (Arlington: American Psycihatric Publishing Inc., 2009), p.10.

they were doing to help you – it was collegiate, you were all in it together – and there was always someone up for being distracted to give you a hand.

However, first you had to get the story, and that was about judgement, instinct, intuition, and making connections. In 1988 I remember one reporter arguing with the news editor that the then health minister Edwina Currie's comment that 'most eggs were infected with salmonella' wasn't much of a story. The editor assured him that it was. The reporter went off unconvinced, and then couldn't get anything out of anyone in the government. Over the next two weeks as the story snowballed and became bigger and bigger, to be one of those unexpected media furores that captures the public imagination, with Edwina Currie being forced to resign as farmers joined forces to mount an attack and march on the government, the poor reporter slunk to the back of the newsroom. He didn't return for further shifts after that, because it was dog eat dog on the news desk, and he had been left, literally, with egg on his face. It was a horribly macho culture. It soon became clear to me that I didn't have the stomach for news, and I would be better off in "fluffy" features.

I decided to try my luck with magazines where the pace wasn't quite so frenetic and the stakes so high. Eschewing the luxury consumerism of the Condé Nast magazines where friends were working – *Tatler*, *Brides*, *House & Garden*, *Vanity Fair*, and *Condé Nast Traveller* – I set up my own magazine (see page 104). Five years on, when I was interviewed for a commissioning editor's job at *The Times*, and brought along copies of my magazine *RASP*, I thought my chances were slim. However, the editor of the Weekend section seemed impressed enough by the enterprise of setting up a magazine, that she hired me on the spot.

The next Monday, I entered the old whisky warehouse in Wapping as Pets, Property, and Shopping Editor for *The Times*, and it felt completely different from my earlier thrashing around in the dark at the *Sunday Express*. I had run my own magazine by then, even sold advertising space, which at *The Times* happened in a different building, so I knew how the whole process of putting together a title worked.

Most importantly, from the very first day, being at *The Times* felt like coming home – the giant window-less warehouse, the mess of the place, with piles of paper on every desk, badly dressed hacks everywhere, and the smoke spiralling up from ashtrays behind them. It was scruffy, it was busy, it was teeming with life, and I loved it from the first intake of breath. On my very first day, I left with a yellow Post-it note stuck to my foot by mistake, and as I looked down at it, I smiled. It seemed to be a sign that this was where I should be.

I used to take the entrance at the far end of the warehouse every morning just so I could pass by every department and mentally prepare for the day. Motoring, Sport, News, Features, Obits, leader writers – there was a hidden pecking order, with News at the top, and yet everyone was on the same floor and seemingly on the same level.

Being connected to everyone in the room meant that *The Times* worked like a collective organism, and there were tribal aspects to their respective corners – the designers wore black and perched at their drawing desks, the younger features writers were put around a table, dubbed "crayon corner" because of their youth, and the subs never ever cracked a smile. (They hated the writers and the editors, because we just gave them extra work.) Everyone had a role, the place hummed with noise, and the smoke from the cigarettes would curl up to the top of the warehouse so that by the end of the day there would be a thick fug for the management at the top.

I didn't just survive there, I flourished. I think it played to all my ADHD qualities, and I took the good fortune of being there seriously. I had ten bosses during my five years on the Weekend section, where I also worked as Food and Drink Editor, Gardening Editor, and Family Travel Editor. Newspapers shift people, relaunch, redesign all the time; it's a restless and reinventing business, and after Murdoch had dispensed with the unions, there was always a threat of the next round of redundancies coming along.

Finally, we moved out of the old whisky warehouse to the award-winning eco-friendly building across the road, and the cramped smoky atmosphere was swapped for new computers that connected to the internet. The thrum and fug of the afternoon was gone, as a more silent atmosphere descended; the beginning of the quieter news offices that was reflected in my last journalistic stint at the *Financial Times*, where nobody used the phones, and you could hear a pin drop.

The Times was a powerful brand, and I launched a number of campaigns while there. The first was to encourage our readers and schools to grow older varieties of vegetables and fruits that had all but disappeared. We sent out seeds of celeriac and black carrots, provided by Heligan Gardens, and created dishes on the Food pages that used these exotic vegetables – it was called the Grow Good Food Campaign. Later, on the property pages we launched a Save our Countryside campaign, which was about preserving the greenbelt and encouraging councils to recover and reuse empty buildings in town instead.

It was creative, and relentless, and I was also appointed Gardening Editor, so hosted tables for the Royal Horticultural Society at the Chelsea Flower Show. I hoped that I wouldn't be uncovered as the imposter who didn't know her azaleas from her dahlias. However, I knew my time was up when the tenth new editor was brought in with a keen interest in horticulture and picked over the individual flowers we had bought her as a bunch in front of me, naming them all in Latin. I realised at that moment that it was just a matter of time before I would be replaced. And when I then found out I was expecting twins, the writing was on the wall.

STRUCTURE VS SELF-EMPLOYMENT

What I didn't realise when I left the office after several years to go on maternity leave, was how precious my position was, and how overwhelming I was going to find being at home, after the relative structure of a job that I loved, and being with colleagues who are still friends today. With journalism, I had found a job where my ADHD qualities seemed to be a boon, rather than an impairment, and I was able to thrive and enjoy the challenge of getting a Saturday newspaper out every week.

However, journalism is also a very public profession, and as I moved over from editing to writing, I found the buck stopped with me. It was my name, not those of the sub-editors, on the piece, so if something went wrong – I was to blame. While at *The Times*, I had written a number of pieces in favour of independent midwives, who had helped with my birth and were under threat over insurance. There was a change made to one of my stories by the sub-editors, and in the process it became skewed towards describing the midwives as "dangerous". It was a big story, involving a leaked government report over a popular London birth centre being closed down, and it was trailed on the front of the newspaper. To explain what had happened – how the story had got skewed – I made the mistake of creating a website and writing my first blog. *The Times* picked up the blog, and asked me to take it down, and I was blacklisted for a good few years. I remember the chill of the news editor calling me and saying, 'We can't force you to take it down, but it is a breach of our employer/employee contract.' I found out I had been blacklisted when I submitted an article commissioned before the incident and a rogue email from a features editor was sent to me by mistake. The email started, "Argggghhhh. Emma Mahony. Can we use her after the blog incident?"

This ability to make giant gaffes in your career, through careless errors or impulsivity, is perhaps one way of sorting out the undiagnosed ADHDer from an occasional blunderbuss. It should be there in the Diagnostic and Statistical Manual, and no doubt a skilled psychiatrist will spot it, because it is proof that when ADHD does show up, it tends to show up big time, especially in your working life. In her memoir, the American author Katherine Ellison wrote about her own early journalism days with undiagnosed ADHD[62]: *When an error I made in a high-profile, death-penalty murder case prompted the $11 million lawsuit ... I'll always be grateful, as well as slightly mystified, that my editors didn't fire me.* Lucky for them that they didn't, because she went on to expose the lavish lifestyles and corruption of the ruling Marcos family in the Philippines, and in so doing won a Pulitzer Prize for investigative journalism. However, she illustrates well how one can hold this ability to shine brilliantly, as well as make "astonishing follies", all at the same desk.

EXECUTIVE MALFUNCTION

Diagnosis and trying medication came too late to save the corporate job that, looking back, I was completely unsuited for, and that came after my *Times* blacklisting. It was my attempt to move from journalism into charity work, something I had taken up voluntarily for a few years while at home with the children, teaching teenage mothers how to cook with the charity Impact Foundation.

My new corporate job was local, it was part-time, and the title was Community Engagement Officer, (which sounded to me as if I got out of the office and wasn't just stuck behind a desk). I had chosen it because this department gave out small grants under £5,000 out of a £150,000 annual fund, as part of their remit, and I thought I would be good at finding good causes to assign the grants. In my usual gung-ho way of expecting everything to turn out right, I thought it would all come good. Instead, it pushed every wrong ADHD button. The part of the job at which I excelled was not where my boss (who was "process" driven and all about mastering the mail-outs on the computer) wished for me to focus. She wasn't interested in ideas or the local community – only the *business* community; and as I came to her with ideas, she described them as 'way above your pay grade'. We clashed horribly.

---

62 Ellison, K, Buzz: *A Year of Paying Attention: A Memoir* (New York: Hyperion, 2012), p26.

I also completely misread how the corporate world worked; this was not a collegiate one like journalism or teaching; you aren't all working together towards a common goal – putting a newspaper out or educating children. In the corporate world, my boss would say to me: 'Notice when you are being slapped down!' (i.e. learn to keep your mouth shut).

One of my first jobs in the corporate office was to create a newsletter, something I had done many times when I had my own publishing company. When I included interesting features of people's good work around the company and worthy causes where the grants were going, my boss elected to replace them with corporate trumpet-blowing. I told her that her version made the newsletter boring to the community, and it would go straight into the bin as a result. That was the beginning of the end.

During this short three-month period, I was still undiagnosed. Although I had started the process with my two meetings with the ADHD specialist nurse, the final interview was yet to take place. The nurse knew that medication could make all the difference to me keeping the job, and was trying to push through my diagnosis as fast as possible.

However, what I wanted to give this company – ideas and connection to the community – was seen as just a pain to my boss and others in the department. People wanted to get by with less work to do, not more, and a new idea meant someone had to do something to make it happen. In this "bog-standard" corporate world, as my boss described it, why would you ever want to add to your workload? As it was explained to me: fresh jobs and directives came from on high. As long as there is a paper trail saying you were on it, why add more work?

I learnt quickly that if you had an idea, hide it until it was almost ready, and then try and finesse it with your boss as a *fait accompli*. She disliked me so much, however, that it rarely worked; she would just pull rank and kill it. Everything came to a head over a competition I had organised to run in the newsletter, 450,000 copies of which were going to be hand-delivered in the area at great expense to the company. The prize was six annual bus passes. which could be won by nominating a community champion.

My rationale was that this was something that would generate positive press in the local community, and also add a feel-good factor to the organisation. My boss blocked it after I had negotiated with the bus company and had the whole thing set up, not least because I had done it behind her back (knowing she would kill it if I told her early on). She removed it from the newsletter, without telling me, and we had a showdown when I found the page proofs changed. She won, of course, because she was my boss, but I was devastated. At the monthly meeting later, when the newsletter was crowned a great success, a fellow colleague was given an award for the newsletter – despite the fact that I had singlehandedly written every story and put it together. It was the last straw, and I knew then I couldn't last long.

Weeks before my diagnosis came through, I went in for an appraisal, where I thought I had met all the objectives set, only to find that I was being fired. My boss, a younger woman whom, despite all of the above, I admired in some ways for her steely toughness, had no interest in my objectives. They were part of an HR box-ticking exercise that had to be in place in order to fire me. She told me I "couldn't be trusted externally" and relayed how a colleague had overheard me quipping to some business partner at a drinks party that I was "finding it hard to move from journalism where you are taught to be precise about things, to the corporate world where you are told to 'inject the right note of vagueness into statements'." I couldn't refute it; they were definitely my words. And she had the final bullet that she needed in her gun to lock and load, and – fire me.

EXECUTIVE FUNCTION

Of course, looking back, it was wholly the wrong environment for someone like myself; everything held dear by them was a challenge for me – *everything*, starting with organisation.

But it also says a lot about how the corporate world embraces neurodiversity. Perhaps my experience shows why so many ADHDers set up on their own[63] ultimately. While the ADHDer might get on with their colleagues, at some point they are going to butt heads with a boss or someone who is so differently wired to them, and they will either have to suppress their personality and withdraw, becoming depressed, or express it and fall out. Add to that mix an impulsive or explosive nature that could lead to storming out anyway, and you can see why the hushed corporate world of everyone in their place isn't going to work for someone with ADHD (without a great amount of compromise).

While my foray into setting up in business in my thirties was a career high point, you can tell from the above account that the corporate job was the exact opposite – a cruel rejection. It left me feeling horrible about myself because being fired is deeply unpleasant, even if you didn't like the place or the people much in the first place. However brave you may be at posturing how you didn't like the job anyway, that nagging sense of "not being good enough" begins to gnaw away, and jokes and jibes at your expense make you feel distrustful of your ability. Now, reflecting on it, I can see that it was completely wrong for someone like myself, and I was desperately trying to bend myself to fit in. Once I had my diagnosis soon after, I could accept that and learn to think about how to use my ADHD traits to my advantage, instead of struggling against them.

[63] Archer, D, *ADHD – the entrepreneur's superpower*, 2014 <https://www.forbes.com/ sites/dalearcher/2014/05/14/adhd-the-entrepreneurs-superpower/#246e692759e9> [accessed 3 August 2018].

CALL TO ACTION

Knowing a lot more about how ADHD affects you, or a loved one, would you consider trying to find yourself or them a job to suit their interests rather than having to bend behaviour to fit the job? For example, knowing that you or they might excel in making connections, or taking risks, or being more active and creative in their work, rather than accepting a quiet desk job, would that inspire you or them to try a more active profession? Many people change their line of work after diagnosis, looking for something more authentic that fits their personality, having struggled to succeed in a career path for a long time. And if you can't be a square peg in a round hole, there is always being your own boss, and creating your own square hole.

CHAPTER 11
RELATIONSHIPS AND FRIENDS

"A good listener is usually thinking about something else."

Kin Hubbard, cartoonist

As we have established, in the adolescent years ADHD shows up differently in girls and boys, and these differences can be seen so clearly in the complicated world of female friendships. Even today, experiments like those carried out in the BBC documentary *A Gender Neutral Education: No More Boys and Girls, Can Our Kids Go Gender Free?* show how little has really changed in a generation. Fifty per cent of boys have good self-esteem, while only 10% of girls report the same. The shock on the adults' faces when they are told that they are pushing boys' toys on a girl (dressed as a boy), or the reverse, shows how strikingly expectations are different between girls and boys as young as seven. Female friendships for most girls and women are a minefield; my experience, growing up with the ADHD, is that I don't have enough fingers to count all the fallings out with friends over some drama.

REJECTION SENSITIVE DYSPHORIA (RSD)

When psychiatrist William Dodson coined this particular phrase for people with ADHD, he set out a stall of some difficult-to-name emotions, which don't usually get talked about. While he also put forward the idea that sometimes the person with ADHD can come across as "cold, insensitive, unaware of the feeling of others"[64], he realised that this was also linked to a hypersensitivity that could lead to a flood and overwhelm of strong emotions. Dr Dodson writes that Rejection Sensitive Dysphoria[65] is the "one emotional condition found only with ADHD"[66]. He describes RSD as a pain that overtakes the person, who then struggles to subdue it. Whether the pain is real or imagined, the intensity of it is brought on by being "rejected, teased, criticised, a disappointment to [themselves or] important people in their lives." Of course everyone can have an extreme reaction to being criticised, but I think it is the amount of criticism that a person with ADHD experiences in their lifetime because of their neurological differences that triggers it, as well as the emotional dysregulation that sits with the disorder. If we return to Kevin Roberts' unexpected answer to the question of what does it feel like to have ADHD (that giant foam finger with the "you're wrong" on it) then you can get some sense of why this "flooding" might take place.

CREATING DRAMA

Add to this sensitivity a paradoxical urge to create a drama, just to stir things up a bit and get the dopamine levels rising, and you can see that a perfect storm can quickly brew in any relationship for the person with ADHD. Then comes the fall-out and the Rejection Sensitive Dysphoria, and the cycle continues. This creation of conflict, this shooting oneself in the foot and then enjoying the hopping around, but not the pain from the wound itself, is part of the complexity of the condition.

---

64 Dodson, W.W., *Emotional Regulation an Rejection Sensitive, Attention magazine*, 2016 <https://chadd.org/wp-content/uploads/2016/10/ATTN_10_16_EmotionalRegulation.pdf> [accessed October 2019].

65 Dodson, W.W., *How ADHD Ignites Rejection Sensitive Dysphoria*, 2020 <https://www.additudemag.com/rejection-sensitive-dysphoria-and-adhd/> [accessed February 2020].

66 Dodson, W.W., *Emotional Regulation an Rejection Sensitive, Attention magazine*, 2016 <https://chadd.org/wp-content/uploads/2016/10/ATTN_10_16_EmotionalRegulation.pdf> [accessed October 2019].

One explanation is that negative situations hold more "juice"; they instigate more brain activity than when life is calm and peaceful; it's the dopamine fix that we crave. This might help to explain why my ADHD son bickers and constantly goads his older brother and twin sister, and our family behind closed doors can some days be a war zone.

As the author and ADHDer Kevin Roberts writes: *ADHD individuals create negative situations and dynamics as one unconscious way to increase cerebral activity … I have come to the inescapable conclusion that I feel more alive when I am being negative. Opposing something gives me more juice than supporting it. We ADHDers create negative dynamics in many areas of our lives … Frequent arguments, broken promises, and insensitive interpersonal styles leave a trail of hurt feelings, disappointments, and bewilderment. ADHDers often exhibit incredible powers of precision in finding ways to push other people's buttons.*

If conflict in our relationships weren't enough, we also can create mayhem in families. Where other families might look forward to returning home as a sanctuary, before Michael and I were diagnosed, home was a place of conflict – conflict that seemed to be started, stoked, or patted down by my son or myself. Once the dust had settled and apologies were finally made, other family members would slink off to their rooms to get away, themselves nursing resentments that still resurface years later. As an extra cruel twist, the person with ADHD may genuinely have little memory of creating the problem in the first place, and so might be slow to make amends.

ANGER AND FRIENDSHIPS

While family members always come back to the table because they have no choice, and learn to deal with the fighting in their own way, friendships and relationships are a far more delicate issue. Sadly, I have been completely dropped by a number of friends over the years because of something I have done or said, usually blurted out or done impulsively, or even seemingly spitefully, with or without awareness. Action rather than reflection has all too often been my *modus vivendi*.

The only thing that most of these incidents had in common (until my diagnosis, that is, when I revisited them with a new understanding) was that they were the other person's fault. Because, until recently, I was a master at pointing the finger elsewhere, often gathering others on my side to stoke up the drama a little, with plausible arguments about why *I* was in the right. Over a lifetime, these spats have sometimes lasted for years, and a few are still unresolved. There's an element of anger and aggression in them, which I think was a protective factor perhaps to keep anxiety and depression at bay. The aggression was radiated outwards, rather than inwards at myself.

Despite the fact that I have now taken the view that I will *never ever* fall out with anyone again (not true, as I have done so while writing this book), I also understand that I am attracted to the slightly madder, badder, and more dangerous-to-know types of people, so I have to work extra hard to make "healthy choices" as my therapist calls it, in my friendships. "We all do our best with the light we have to see with, but sometimes that light is not very bright," is an Alcoholics Anonymous saying that I have taken to heart. I now try to confine the drama in my life to an acting class, or my theatre and film production company, as a way of subverting that need into a more harmless form.

THE WIDER COMMUNITY

Impulsivity can be a problem with those who don't know you. For example, when we moved to the country, I managed to fall out with the whole village in one fell swoop by writing an article that the sub-editors entitled: "Stuck in the Sticks: the misery of the countryside". To be fair to myself, I was stitched up by the headline writers at *The Times*; nevertheless, it was me who landed myself firmly in it. Alongside that headline of "Stuck in the Sticks[67]" appeared a picture of me, looking rain-splashed and suitably dishevelled after three rejected photocalls that day.

67 Mahony, E, *Stuck in the Sticks*, 2008 <https://www.thetimes.co.uk/article/stuck-in-the-sticks-5zkhhvq5zdg> [accessed January 2020].

Overnight, I became a pariah in the parish. This was also before *The Times* went behind the online paywall, so the comments that appeared beneath the piece added insult to self-injury. Angry country folk ranted about everything from the arrogance of DFLs (Down From Londoners) to the hatred of metropolitan uppitiness. It was a faux pas that even now continues to haunt me, as not much happens in our little village in Sussex, and what I thought was a light-hearted article, tossed off in an afternoon, circulated around the village faster than an Australian bushfire.

I quickly found myself skulking around our new neighbourhood, asking my neighbour to walk the twins up to school, and while I didn't receive bullets in the letterbox (like one female journalist who had to move back to London from Dartmoor in Devon after writing her 'How I Came to Hate My Hideaway' piece), I did continue to get confronted about the article at the most unexpected of times.

Although I realised quickly that this wasn't the London approach that I was used to – where gossip and fashion move on so quickly that yesterday's news is already forgotten – I was genuinely unaware that my act of self-sabotage would follow me around for years to come.

Local friends also began to fall away when it came to lift-sharing (something that few bothered to do, which I also couldn't understand, and had mentioned foolishly in the article as being un-ecological). Because driving everywhere seemed to be the norm in the countryside, I would offer a fetch-and-return for the after-school run or activities, as we had done in London, where most mothers worked. But in the country, fuel-heavy 4x4s roared around the hedgerows picking up one small child, and mothers rarely worked so collecting their kids became their job. While I continued to freelance from home, I might occasionally be late to pick up their children on my school run, so any lift-share arrangements would suddenly be dropped, and I would suffer the latest round of rejection.

So, I blamed the rural community for their lack of environmental awareness around lift-sharing, and then expected the mothers to be a little more laid-back about getting their children back at a given moment. Until my diagnosis, this was my traditional sort of battle hymn: 'What a waste of petrol and time!' I railed. 'What's wrong with everyone?' I would fulminate against the local bus company, ringing them to ask why they only had a bus that arrived in the middle of the day, effectively making it useless for school times?

I even sent my eldest son off to school on a bicycle, which prompted one woman in the playground to call me a "cruel mother" and, soon after, I received a letter from the headmaster stating that the school held no responsibility: "We don't encourage bicycling," he said, "as it could lead to carnage on the roads". Once again, I seemed at loggerheads with everyone around us. My defence was always to go on the offence, even when they were in the wrong, not me.

Perhaps what wasn't obvious in my aggressive stance was how much I truly cared about being at odds with everyone else. My husband – still commuting daily to London and now not home before 8.30 pm every night – fortunately thought my "pariah" status was funny. Like the time I was late to pick up my daughter and ran over someone's cat while speeding, it remains as one of his favourite dinner party stories – how we moved down from London at my insistence and then became the damned of the village. But I was having to suffer the daily slings and arrows at the school gates, mixed with the paranoia that I was going to be verbally set upon by someone in a car park, so almost wanted to move back to London again. I felt cruelly rejected, but I only had myself to blame.

EMOTIONAL AFFAIRS

There's another aspect of ADHD that can potentially cause problems in relationships and that's the idea of emotional affairs. It's almost like a form of hyperfocus (see page 33) applied to a relationship, and there is some talk in Melissa Orlov's writing of a "hyperfocus courtship"[68], where the partner is wined and dined

---

[68] Orlov, M, Kohlenberger, N, *The Couple's guide to Thriving with ADHD* (Forest Lake: LMFT Specialty Press 2019).

and paid so much attention by the ADHD future spouse, that they have little idea of what a true relationship will look like once the novelty has worn off, and the dopamine rush of falling in love has been swopped for the "deep, deep peace of the marital bed". I'd never heard the term "emotional affairs" until I read the author Tim Lott's article in *The Times* about discovering his ADHD aged sixty-one, and writing about how emotional affairs had affected his marriage[69].

Relate, the marriage guidance counselling organisation in the UK, defines emotional affairs as *that grey area where you know you're more than just platonic friends with someone outside of your relationship. There's an emotional connection, an intimacy and often an attraction – to each other – even if there is no physical or sexual interaction between the two of you.*

Often, this non-sexual relationship will be described as a "friendship", but you are pursuing it with an unbalanced intention (sometimes unaware). While these "affairs" are usually with the opposite sex, they are not always, and the difference between an "emotional affair" and a "friendship" is that the former can be troublesome for a number of reasons.

Melissa Orlov, the author of *The ADHD Effect on Marriage*, writes on her blog[70]: *with an emotional affair there is a "tug" that you know, if you are honest with yourself, shouldn't be there. There is a "lightness" and an eagerness to be with a person that you don't feel with others who are just friends. And a hallmark of emotional affairs is that they interfere with your current relationship – either right now or having the potential to do so in the future.*

These "emotional affairs" are more common in people with ADHD; around half or 49% of women with ADHD admitted to having emotional affairs while in a committed relationship, as opposed to 36% of women without ADHD. There is a wider gap for men, 43% of men with ADHD (versus 25% of men

---

[69] Lott, T, *Am I too old to have ADHD?*, 2017 <https://www.thetimes.co.uk/article/am-i- too-old-to-have-adhd-76czn8gkl> [accessed October 2018].

[70] Orlov, M, *Are You Having an Emotional Affair? Is Your Partner Having an Emotional Affair??*, 2016 <https://www.adhdmarriage.com/content/are-you-having-emotional-affair- your-partner-having-emotional-affair> [accessed October 2019].

without it) according to research by Ari Tuckman[71], an American psychologist and sex therapist specialising in ADHD, who surveyed 3,000 people with ADHD and their non-ADHD partners.

The survey results were published in his book[72] in 2019. Elaborating on the results, Tuckman said, *In my survey of couples with one ADHD partner, I asked two separate questions about infidelity: 1. physical hookups without an emotional connection 2. emotional affairs that may or may not have a physical component … So, when I said emotional affairs in my survey, it may or may not have included a physical component, which is an important difference if it does or doesn't. Therefore, the percentages I came up with are a mix of those two experiences, as opposed to purely emotional affairs.*

Tuckman went on to say: *People engage in physical and/or emotional infidelity for lots of reasons, not all of which are a response to an unhappy relationship. However, an unhappy relationship does increase the risks, especially if the unhappiness seems insurmountable. A couple who has not yet found a way to resolve the challenges associated with ADHD or to negotiate their other differences may therefore be more tempted to stray. If one isn't getting their needs met by their partner, it's tempting to seek those needs in others. Or to be willing to let something gradually slide across the line of appropriateness. While this can provide some temporary stability to the primary relationship if it drains off some of the discontent, it also tends to siphon off the motivation to actually make things better in the relationship. And if the infidelity is discovered, it can create a lot of hurt and blow up the relationship. The obvious advice is to invest that energy into improving the primary relationship or to make the conscious choice to end the relationship before starting something new. Easy to say; harder to do.*

I would add to the reasons he gives a few extra, such as: the thrill of the chase; the problems in one's own relationship caused by the undiagnosed ADHD (bit of drama), and the intensity, interest, and attention that comes with the novelty of a new "friendship". While I can honestly say I have never had a physical affair during my long monogamous relationships,

---

71 Tuckman, A, https://tuckmanpsych.com/

72 Tuckman, A, *ADHD After Dark: Better Sex Life, Better Relationship* (New York: Routledge, 2019).

I've definitely had a few emotional ones. The only difference perhaps between myself, and those for whom a relationship has broken down, is that I have had the benefit of therapy, as well as couples counselling along the way, to keep the wheels on the domestic cart.

TEN THINGS ABOUT AN ADHD FRIENDSHIP

My old university friend Clarissa Vorfeld, who lives in Switzerland and has known me for over thirty years, highlights the challenges and rewards of an ADHD friendship.

Challenges:

1) Timing: Emma's sense of time is not the same as yours or your other anxious watch-checking friends. If you do miss that train, her take is 'Relax! So what? You can always catch another.' So, if we are travelling together, I need to take charge of time planning.

2) Essentials: We all know that certain material things are fairly key to a smooth-running life – a phone, switched on and with enough battery; house keys; wallet, laptop. Your ADHD friend can somehow manage without these things and they don't use the ritual checks that we non-ADHDers do – have I got my phone or credit card? So sometimes you actually need to see the phone or card with your own eyes to avoid the 'I'm sure it was in my bag' scenario.

3) Mislaying things: We won't call it losing, as they are rarely lost, just left somewhere on a shelf, on a shop counter, on a train seat. So, when I'm with Emma, I always check when we get up from the table in a bar that nothing's been left on the chair or the tabletop. Recently, in a Portuguese market, Emma installed me in a café to read, while she spent an hour thoughtfully shopping all the market stalls for well-chosen presents for family and friends. When we finally met up, where were her bags of gifts? Oh dear! It turned out that a moment's distraction while paying for some cheap cotton underpants had meant she had left all her morning's shopping somewhere in the market. Needless to say, I was really upset for her, but she wasn't much bothered and soon forgot all about it.

4) Displaced anxiety: While the ADHD friend may not sweat what they see as "small stuff", the close friend often will. Emma arrived by plane to visit me only to announce that she had accidentally travelled on her daughter's passport instead of her own. She had managed to sail through passport control with a passport showing her as a blonde sixteen-year-old schoolgirl. She didn't give it a second thought. Meanwhile I spent the weekend in a tense ball of anxiety wondering whether she would be arrested or prevented from leaving come Sunday night.

5) Support As with all close relationships, you are often called on for support and counsel by your ADHD friend. Here, you have to suspend your own personal approach and try to empathise with hers as it often diverges strongly from what you or any non-ADHD person would do. Take her occasional fall-outs: a widely held view would be to "let it go". Just apologise, smile, and move on. But. 'Hey!' she will say, 'I'm not going to lie down and just take it. He/she needs to be told how I feel, and apologise for *their* mistake.' For Emma, there may be something cleansing about having it out. For many of us, this is a situation to be avoided at all costs.

Rewards:

6) Carefree: I've learnt what "carefree" really looks like through my friendship with Emma. Typical example: It's getting late, I worry. We won't have enough time to get to the shops, drop off the birthday present and so on. That's what you and I think, with always a watchful eye on the time and on plans. The ADHDer in my experience is free from these constraints. Spontaneity is key and if you're along for the ride, you might have to stop by the sea and rush in for a dip. Who knows?

7) Parking problems: This situation would never have happened to me: Emma drove a couple of hours to see a friend's play in a small town and, not finding any street parking, just popped the car in a garage near the theatre. I would have stopped, checked that it was an all-night garage and open to the public. But not Emma. After the performance, she found the garage firmly locked for the night, leaving her with no way of getting home. No big deal, right? You just have to find the nearest motel and stay the night. This would have thrown me completely, but not our ADHD friends. Water off a duck's back.

8) Living in the now: I now see that constant awareness of timing and planning often means you're not in the present moment. My experience of a friend with ADHD is that they are always in the now, so much so that other plans go awry. If that sunset is worth stopping for, or those apples look ripe for picking, then who cares if you're trying to get to the supermarket before it closes? Things will turn out alright.

9) Generosity: The largeness of life and all its pleasures that an ADHD friend experiences, that lack of nit-picking scrupulousness, goes hand-in-hand with an easy generosity. This person is not counting who had the steak and who had the tomato salad. Who cares? Let me pay for it! Whether they're flush with money or not makes no difference – they're happy to bring out the credit card (if they haven't lost it, that is) and pay up, rarely remembering to ask for repayment.

10) We can learn from them: I have learnt through my friendship with Emma to take things as they come. It'll all turn out okay. And they prove that life can be lived in a more uninhibited, impulsive way. I loathe people dropping in unannounced, but I'm pretty certain you could knock on Emma's door anytime and she'd welcome you in and put the kettle on. ADHDers can indulge a fancy, stop and smell the flowers, have a chat with a needy friend: it somehow seems more free, more joyful. Find yourself an ADHD friend – I recommend it!

CALL TO ACTION

If you are vulnerable to emotional affairs, or your partner has ADHD and you can see this tendency in them, Relate recommends seeing this as symptomatic of something that is missing or going wrong in your original relationship. "Discovering an emotional affair can be an opportunity to look at this with couple counselling" suggests the marriage guidance counselling service. The benefit of an emotional affair over a physical one is that there is still plenty of opportunity to salvage the good that exists in the relationship, rather than drag the same problems into a new one.

CHAPTER 12
PARENTHOOD

"It seems impossible to lean in, without falling over."
Parent with ADHD

There is relatively little research on the effect of ADHD on parenting, but as you can imagine, distraction, impulsivity, and lack of organization or planning (executive functioning is the grand term) don't make for a quiet and smoothly run household.

In some studies[73], there is a documented lack of household routines or emotionally impulsive and negative responses to the child (like pushing your ADHD preschooler off his chair as he pours a pint of water into your cooking bowl – see page 198). These studies conclude that "collectively, these suboptimal approaches to parenting interact with and are linked to negative child outcomes". Yikes. As I read these, I hope that the presence of a father, and an extra adult around to help with childcare from time to time, offset these findings that reduce the sometimes messy business of parenting to "suboptimal approaches". On top of this guilt, is the guilt matched by other working mothers, who probably weren't around much in their children's early days. I was working from home with my twins, so was around but obviously clinically distracted.

The authors of different studies[74] found that parents with ADHD assessed themselves as having higher rates of stress

---

[73] Safren, S.A., Sprich S, Chulvick S, Otto, M.W., Psychosocial treatments for adults with attention-deficit/hyperactivity disorder. *Psychiatr Clin North Am.*27(2), (2004) pp.349–360.

[74] Barkley, R.A., Murphy, K.R., Fischer M, *ADHD in adults: What the science says* (New York: Guilford, 2008).

compared to general population samples, and lower parenting confidence independent of their child's problems. This makes sense to me, because being pulled in more than one direction is stressful, and the usual coping mechanisms for someone with ADHD can easily collapse under the weight of having two (or three) equally urgent focuses. The "lower parenting confidence" speaks to past brushes with failure and repeated mistakes, so there is already a lack of self-belief in how to do things. Add to this the early years' preoccupation with baby "milestones" and comparing yourself (as a parent) and your baby (those NCT groups and growth and weight charts), and it is easy to see how quickly a mother with ADHD can feel wanting. And I say mother because figures show that despite the rise in fathers staying at home over the last twenty-five years, the UK reflects many modern Western countries with the figures representing 223,000 fathers at home, as opposed to 1,819,000 mothers.

Perhaps more worrying is where the studies find that parents with ADHD offer "lax discipline" and what they call "over-reactive parenting", suggesting a mother with ADHD relates "to more inconsistent discipline, more inappropriate repetition of commands, and more negative parenting control (criticism, physical punishment)[75]". Double yikes. In 2004, Section 58 of the Children's Act in the UK made it unlawful to smack a child "except where this amounts to 'reasonable punishment'", a legally defined phrase, with each case considered if it came to this. It was also made illegal for anyone else to smack a child without parental consent, and organisations such as the NSPCC are calling for an all-out ban on smacking. Such studies show that ADHD parents, with impulse and anger issues, can be completely at odds with current social norms.

---

[75] Chronis-Tuscano, A, Raggi, V.L., Clarke, T.L., Rooney, M.E., Diaz, Y, Pian J, 'Associations between maternal attention-deficit/hyperactivity disorder symptoms and parenting', *Journal of Abnormal Child Psychology*, 36, (2008) pp.1237–1250.

However, it's not all bad. One study[76] showed that parenting an ADHD child when you have ADHD yourself was "unexpectedly associated with more positive parenting", and compared it with parents without ADHD inflicting more negative parenting (both self-reported and observed). It suggests that this might be down to a natural empathy with the behaviours of the child, and a match for the cognitive tempo of the child – perhaps choosing another trip to the park for more swinging on the swing, instead of getting the dreaded homework done.

It is still too early to know the social impact on parenting an ADHD child when you have ADHD yourself, but you can at least take some succour from the fact that we know poor parenting is not the cause of the ADHD in the first place. The fact that an ADHD child is often described as the result of poor parenting, however, will just compound the shaky self-esteem of a parent with ADHD in the first place. To counter some of the negative messages received in a neurotypical world, an ADHD child needs more positive ones at home, and an advocate who knows that he or she is trying and doing the best they can is more likely to be an understanding parent with ADHD, than the other half who is at their wits' end.

YOUNG MOTHERHOOD

I had fallen pregnant by mistake with a boyfriend at the age of nineteen, when I was on the pill. I had made up a big story about how I must have been the 0.1% that was able to get pregnant on the pill, and how I was extremely fertile, but now, looking back post-diagnosis, I had probably just forgotten to take it[77]. When I found out I was pregnant, I was shocked. I was just out of school and it was before university, so this wasn't even a path I considered

---

[76] Psychogiou, L, Daley, D, Thompson, M, Sonuga-Barke, E, 'Testing the interactive effect of parent and child ADHD on parenting in mothers and fathers: A further test of the similarity-fit hypothesis', *British Journal of Developmental Psychology*. 25, (2007) pp. 419–433.

[77] Skoglund, C, Kopp, K.H., Skalkidou, A, et al. Association of Attention-Deficit/Hyperactivity Disorder With Teenage Birth Among Women and Girls in Sweden. JAMA Netw Open. 2019;2(10):e1912463. doi:10.1001/jamanetworkopen.2019.12463

possible. I belonged to the first generation to have control over our bodies, and I exercised it without much thought.

I didn't realise then that I was in a statistical majority of girls with ADHD who fall pregnant as teenagers, as a recent Swedish study observes: *Although teenage pregnancies are a rare occurrence in women and girls in Sweden with or without ADHD, as suggested by an overall rate of teenage deliveries of 3.0% in this study, women and girls with ADHD were associated with a six-fold increased risk for teenage birth compared with women and girls without ADHD and contributed 8.4% to all teenage births. This is evident despite the widespread availability of contraception in Sweden.* Presumably this is down to the risky behaviour of girls with ADHD.

I knew instinctively that becoming a mother at such an early age would put all career and educational future plans on hold, and yet I had still fallen pregnant. I was about to find out that having a termination is a shameful experience. There are the necessary hoops to jump through, being signed off by two doctors, the clinics that specialise in it – the stirrups, the lying about your reasons, the awkward questions, the waiting room, in some misnamed place – usually called the Family Centre – knowing that you and everyone else is there for the wrong reason.

The whole experience has to be dealt with quickly, hushed up, and never spoken about again. And yet the grief, anger, remorse, and sorrow for a life not lived hangs around for months after the deed is done. And then, in my case, you go and make the same mistake all over again. Twice. The last time I asked to be fully conscious for the termination, a form of degradation and self-torture in the hope that I would never get myself into this situation again. Forgetting, of course, that it always takes two to tango.

Before I turned fifty, I began volunteering with teenage mothers, teaching them how to cook. I was drawn to this group because I had so much respect for their decision to go ahead with the pregnancy, whereas when I was their age, I didn't have the guts. They've helped me to understand why some *would* choose motherhood early. Having a baby to love, and a baby that loves you back, is a big thing in the lives of these girls, particularly if they missed out on feeling a mother's love in their early family upbringing. Most of the teenagers I worked with had complicated family lives, at least a couple of them clearly had undiagnosed ADHD, and none of them had cared much for school. Being a mother was their way of having a place in the world, and their decision to go ahead with a pregnancy offered an identity and a purpose, and straightened out their lives in some way.

This was something that they chose to do, often against the wishes of their family, which is why they were living in supported housing, a refuge of sorts. The fact that they are viewed so negatively by society, at worse described as feckless ne'er-do-wells trying to get a place on the social housing ladder, is completely unfair. I found their courage in choosing the road less travelled, and nurturing a new human being was something brave, done instinctively; walking around with a child on their hip without the fear and neuroticism that surrounded my generation who came to motherhood late. Far from being feckless, they were brilliant mums, devoted to their babies, as their interest in knowing how best to feed them healthily, showed. By the end of my five years, the young mothers were growing vegetables in the communal garden, making bread from scratch every cooking session, and teaching the new intake the rules of the kitchen (based on the 1-2-3 Magic programme, which teaches behaviour to young ADHD children. If they swore in the kitchen, they were put on a 1. At a 3 they had to take a time-out based on how old they were.)

LATE MOTHERHOOD

By the time I had my first child in my early thirties, I never realised how messy and urgent the occupation would be, how the sleeplessness of early babyhood would become a form of torture, how lives that can no longer be ordered by the rhythm of 9 to 5 feel like they are literally unravelling. In a way, I was fortunate. I had the means to carry on working part-time at *The Times*, so I could afford to have help. Because straddling the gap between what I was able to do and what was expected – getting first my eldest, and then later the twins, out of the door, with me looking reasonably like the rest of the working population, seemed nigh on impossible.

What I loved most about motherhood was pregnancy and birth – usually the part that most women abhor. For me the hormonal surge was a tonic to my disordered brain, and for the first time in my life I felt at peace and whole. With a baby on board, suddenly I was purposeful, important, and felt I was doing something wonderful all the time – growing new life. This was the same for both pregnancies. The cumbersome burden of carrying twins was far outweighed by this great hormonal injection, coupled with the knowledge that there was no higher purpose, no greater job than this. A calm and quiet descended in pregnancy like no other period in my life. I could function, I felt well, I felt highly intuitive, I was able to check in with myself and make decisions without falling into a usual state of uncertainty. I even looked forward to the birth, like a marathon runner looks forward to a big race.

The birth of my twins normally, without a proposed C-section, was most definitely the best experience in my life, a physical expression that could never be repeated nor bettered. I was on a high from it for weeks after, nothing could compare to this, bringing forth two new lives into the world, and sticking two fingers up to the naysayers who said I had to do it in a hospital by C-section.

BABYHOOD

I recount these two opposite sides of the same coin, termination and birth, because, for me, they represent the negatives and positives of ADHD for women specifically. There are plenty of supporting statistics to show that girls with ADHD are more likely to take more risks with their fertility[78], with the latest longitudinal study suggesting they are twice as likely as their neurotypical peers to fall pregnant before the age of twenty. The study also showed that the ADHD group fell pregnant younger,

[78] Hua M-H, et al., *'Early Pregnancy Risk Among Adolescents With ADHD: A Nationwide Longitudinal Study'* Journal of Attention Disorders. (2020), https://doi.org/10.1177/1087054719900232

and more frequently, with only the use of medication for ADHD lowering the risk.

In my five years of teaching the teen mums to cook, it was also clear that many of their decisions to go ahead and have a baby were driven by complicated forces, and while I had nothing but admiration for the courage of these young mothers, and awe for their total commitment to their babies, I wasn't able to do the same at such a young age. However, at the end of our cooking sessions together, when we would lay the table with a tablecloth and flowers, put out cutlery, and all sit around the table with babies and toddlers squished between us in their highchairs, differences did show up for how much harder their lives might be for choosing this path. Some of the girls admitted to never sitting around a table at home to eat, or even having one in their family, and social workers, midwives, health visitors, young fathers, and the support worker, Anne, would often join us at the table to eat the lunch they had made.

The support worker sometimes credited the cooking sessions as helping the young mothers to keep hold of their babies when social workers were circling, forming an opinion of whether the babies should be taken into care. I hoped the social workers would leave the refuge with a favourable impression of the teenagers' commitment to being mothers and showing how they could get the basics right, nurturing their child. However, it was a reminder of how precarious their choices sometimes were, especially when during my time there two babies were withdrawn from their care – leaving the mothers to go haywire from the stress.

On more than one occasion, I witnessed the breakdown that followed having their baby taken away, which led me to conclude that this kind of state intervention was utterly wrong. What these mothers needed was more support, not a punishment that worked for neither mother or child. I understood how hard it was to navigate the overwhelm of early motherhood, the sleeplessness, the worry, the total loss of self-hood as you subverted your own needs to a bawling, bewildering bundle, so I was drawn to their courage. They never wanted to give up their child, and it seemed plain wrong that they could be made to – just because of a low IQ, or a report from some other service about the mother's behaviour. I had had all the help a mother could hope for in the early days, and yet it took these teenagers' honest, stripped-back approach to remind me what a precious and important job motherhood is. When social services considered they had "acted in the best interest of the child" by removing the baby, they didn't really acknowledge that a mother and baby are one. What is the cost to society of putting a baby in care, particularly when the mother usually goes off the rails immediately afterwards, having lost her whole purpose cruelly and suddenly? After that, they are deemed unlikely to have the baby restored to them, despite the obvious reason for their acting out. I left the refuge when I started to teach, and no longer had time to volunteer, and the experience really added perspective to the difficult pupils in my class. I wanted to persist with the teenage girls particularly because I could see the benefits of keeping them in education as long as possible. If only so they could grow up to challenge the decisions of those who professed to know better about their bodies and their babies.

TODDLERHOOD

When Michael was four years old, after his kindergarten teacher told me she thought he might have ADHD, I went out of my way to deny it. I refused a home visit by a health visitor, said that I would get him tested privately, hoping perhaps to control the final answer. As any proper denial story goes, it would be three years before I did get him tested, having whipped him out of that nursery soon after. I suppose it is a natural reaction to defend your child, or to not want there to be any mental health issue, but when I look back on it, I can see a pattern with anyone who crossed me in this way: I rubbished them. Plus, as my own ADHD was still undiagnosed, and I shared a certain amount of behavioural traits with Michael, I genuinely didn't understand what all the fuss was about. Nowadays, if ever anyone says to me, 'The teacher says this about my child ... what do *you* think?'

I reply, '*Listen* to the teachers.' Because I didn't, I was still at war with authority, and neglected to get Michael the extra support he would have received if I had listened in the first place.

And yet, when I look back on some diary entries from that time, (see appendix) I can see that it is written there in black ink on white paper. Oh, how powerful is the force of denial.

CALL TO ACTION

As a mother, I was lucky to be able to use the need to work from home during the early years of my twins to get extra home help. However, if you have ADHD or even suspect you have it, I would *always* suggest getting more support. Many people with ADHD often *think* they should be able to keep their house in order like others, but the challenges of this brain-based disorder will prove otherwise. There should be no stigma or shame around asking for more help, whether that's from grandparents or other relatives, or paid. Motherhood and managing the emotions around it is extremely challenging for those with ADHD in the family, and unless your partner is supporting you well to live in a happy but chaotic household, getting extra help is a necessity rather than a luxury.

CHAPTER 13
ON THE MOVE AGAIN

"Life is like riding a bicycle. To keep your balance you must keep moving."
Albert Einstein

The holy trinity of ADHD symptoms, as you may already be able to recite off by heart already, are impulsivity, distractibility, and restlessness. Of these, possibly restlessness is talked about the least in adults, because the fidgetiness associated with childhood ADHD often recedes as one ages. That is thought to be one of the reasons why Adult ADHD didn't exist until relatively recently. However, that restlessness often internalises into a mental restlessness, or in my case it manifested in another way: moving house. And with moving house, often comes moving your children in and out of schools, so once you start to look at restlessness in that context, you can see how it can impact on adult life.

MOVING FOR THE SAKE OF IT

Pre-diagnosis, moving house was something I did at the drop of a hat. People say that sharks die if they don't keep moving; they need motion. For me, moving house was progress; it was the promise of something new, something better: new neighbours, the niceness that goes with being new neighbours, the novelty of a different neighbourhood, new restaurants, new supermarkets, new people. However, moving comes at a cost, the least of which is financial. It is complicated, it involves forms, and deposits, and regulations, and cleaning curtains, and other challenging bores in life. If not executed properly, it leaves a trail of pissed off people, or, at best, just the odd two or three.

Moving also has an unexpected emotional impact on those left behind, and it creeps into their dealings with you when you announce it. I could tell there was something wrong with a friend's marriage when our move prompted a card to say how keen she was that they weren't "forgotten" when we moved. Of course I wasn't abandoning her, but it felt like it to her in the circumstances that were about to unravel. People take moving personally, they assume it might have something to do with them, it brings up uncomfortable feelings about the place you are moving from as somehow lesser, especially when some of the moves we've made over the years seem a bit incomprehensible (and looking back are).

It looks like I like to move for the sake of moving, and perhaps before the diagnosis I did. Most people list moving house on the stress scale along with death and divorce, but since getting married, and before diagnosis, we moved house around fifteen times – nearly always prompted by me. What must it be like to be married to someone that peripatetic?

This has also involved a lot of renting, which I don't even like. With renting, it never felt like our house was our home – we weren't allowed to have pets or put up pictures on the wall. When we decided to rent a stable block on someone's country estate and move out of London for the first time, before our first child was born, it was a move too far. Besides the rent, we suddenly had train fares to add on, plus the time spent commuting. Suddenly working in London became an obstacle course to get through every day, even if the fields and wildflowers made it an adventure. So while my eldest son had his first few months of babyhood in a pram pushed up country lanes, it wasn't long before we moved back from the country to London, something apparently nobody ever does.

There followed more house moves, as we house-sat for a friend in Surrey while we tried to buy in South West London. Eventually we managed to buy a tiny flat in Duntshill Road in London, a flat so small that you couldn't lay a yoga mat anywhere. This upstairs railway-worker's cottage in Earlsfield was seemingly made of cardboard, and the flat had a medieval proximity to the neighbours. After one of our regular marital arguments, the woman living downstairs and across the fence came running out into her garden to ask if our neighbour below us was alright (such was the close quarters in which we lived). 'I heard the shouting and was worried about you,' she called across the fence. Meanwhile, I was crouching stricken with embarrassment below the window-sill out of view, waving frantically at my husband to keep his voice down.

Miraculously, some good friends moved in next door to us, also upstairs, so we could plug in our baby alarm and join them for supper while listening out for any snuffling noise through the wall. One night my husband fell asleep on their spare bed after drinking too much at dinner, and was woken by our eldest son crying in his cot through the wall.

With a small inheritance after the death of my uncle, we put down a bigger deposit and traded up, this time to a Victorian four-bedroom semi – just before the year 2000. It felt hopeful and spacious and finally like a family house; somewhere substantial, even if slugs came up through the stripped floorboards because the ground floor was over a tributary of the River Wandle. The twins were born in this house, which was soon traded for another up the road, in search of better primary schools.

MOVING SCHOOLS

If we weren't moving house, I was probably moving the three children into a different school. By the time we moved to the country (for the second time), my eldest son at the age of ten was making his fifth school move, and the twins who were six were on to their third school. As well as my own restlessness, there was also something else going on. I was on a quest to keep Michael's behaviour under the radar after the ADHD comment by his nursery teacher, and every new school would start with the desire to settle Michael quickly, with much goodwill and attention invested.

We didn't make it into one of the better state primaries in the London borough of Wandsworth, so the twins attended a primary school called Swaffield, a place shunned at the time by the sharp-elbowed middle-class mothers in the borough. The twins were put in separate classes, because that was the school's "twin policy" (research has now proved this is not always for the best), and they had the full-on busy London school experience, with after-school clubs and PTA sales daily and weekly, and committed young teachers in classes bursting with thirty children.

After the nursery teacher's ADHD comment, I was on tenterhooks – but the first year of school came and went, with two mature and experienced teachers in a diverse class, at least half of whom had English as a second language. The teachers didn't seem to be phased by anything; at the parents' evening one teacher told me with a slight smile: 'We couldn't find Michael one day, until we looked under the table and there he was, sniffing his blanket!' In a blizzard of potato prints in that wonderful reception year, he seemed to get through. And nobody told me how he had broken the drainpipe on the side of the school by swinging off it in his first week. In fact, I later learnt that Michael was quite often in the head teacher's office. Perhaps because of Swaffield's most famous former pupil, world-class heavyweight boxer Frank Bruno, the school didn't seem to mind a bit of rough-and-tumble.

However, as is often the case, in Year One things took a different turn. A young female teacher, for whom discipline was more of an issue, assigned him individual behaviour targets and education plans. He was given a "rocket chart" to fill in daily – a move that was so successful, I begged subsequent teachers to use it.

What I noticed when I went into his class to listen to the children read is that while the other children seemed to be engrossed with what was in front of them, Michael kept coming up to me and advising me on each child's reading level, and which book they had last read. 'It should be a purple book, Mummy,' he'd say, 'because Milan has finished the red level', or 'Osama has read *Biff and Chip Go to the Library* already, Mummy.' While the other kids seemed in their own world, he seemed awake to every person in that room – reminding me how to pronounce their names properly, or showing me where their reading folders were kept. He was more teaching assistant than pupil, and I saw it as pure enthusiasm. However, the teacher asked me not to read in his class after this, because Michael was deemed "too excited" when I did.

In Michael's second year, the teacher was strict with Michael, who didn't like her much, and she refused to give him any special treatment as she sashayed around the class, resplendent in her colourful sari. 'We don't do rocket charts in Year Two,' she explained to me when I pleaded with her to try one. 'We expect more mature behaviour.' Meanwhile, his twin sister Millie in the next-door class was flourishing, and being offered a creative writing programme in her lunch break for a handpicked few. I tried not to compare.

Then the innocence of the primary years faded suddenly when a boy who had punched my elder son after school brought a knife into school the following day. I was asked to write a letter to support his exclusion. Suddenly the need for good secondary schools and the prospect of Michael getting drawn into the pre-teen conflict, made me worry. Perhaps it was time for another move.

MOVE TO THE COUNTRY

By the time we moved to the country in search of better secondary schools, the twins were turning seven. We found a good private school for my eldest, and in the sleepy rural backwater of the village, the primary school seemed perfectly peaceful, with plenty of playground space and a quarter of the pupils of the noisy Swaffield. I met the temporary head teacher and took Michael down for the day, where he had lunch, which was cooked fresh. The school was a short walk from our new house.

Another benefit of moving schools so often was the tendency to put misbehaviour down to "settling in". Add to that the fact that there was always a sense of excitement around "twins" joining the school. My first spat in the new village primary, before the publication of the article (see page 129), was a reaction to how few activities were offered, after the bustle and busy schedule at Swaffield in London, where the children had tons of after-school options. In our rural backwater, there were almost no activities on offer, little sport, no breakfast clubs, not even regular reading with the children – a ritual performed by two parents every day, for half an hour, at drop-off time in London.

So, I offered to read to the children … and was put outside the twins' class for more than two hours as every child brought me their book one at a time. Some books had not been changed for months – one child even had a book with no words inside. I was shocked. By Year One in London, every child was read to daily, books were changed daily, and their reading level – even for children who joined in that year without English as a first language – was good. Here in the shires, where none of the children had English as a second language, some pupils had books with no words in them. How was that even possible?

I complained to the head teacher, and asked if a better reading programme could be organised, citing the example of their London school, and he seemed to agree without offering to do anything about it. Halfway through my complaint, he brought in my twins' new teacher, who was visibly annoyed to be included. I had already made an enemy there, it seemed.

MOVE BACK TO TOWN

One afternoon in October, Michael came home with a bunch of handwritten notes in his bag. On each side of the paper, in the childish handwriting of each of his classmates, and underneath an "unhappy face" were comments about Michael, specifically what they didn't like about him. "Michael pushes in the playground," said one. "He shouts out a lot", said another. "He is rude", came a third. "He swears sometimes", said another classmate. You could tell from the bundle of notes that this was an exercise that a teacher had made the children do, and that the odd child felt troubled by it. One had mitigated the negative comment by saying: "He is noisy but can be funny". Twenty-nine notes, with twenty-nine negative comments, and on the reverse was a smiley face with what they liked about him. Of course, the positive comments weren't the ones remembered.

It hurts when I think of the shock of finding those notes in his bag, even today. 'What an earth was going on?' was my first question. Michael explained that the head teacher had taken it upon himself to ask the class to do this exercise, because Michael had upset a game of Monopoly during 'wet play', and shouted at an older boy.

The head teacher wasn't even there when the incident prompting the punishment had happened, but had taken Michael out of lunch and spent an hour with him in his office. Then they both went back into his classroom, and the head teacher interrupted the class, saying: 'I'd like everyone in the class to write down what they like *and don't like* about Michael, under a smiley and unhappy face.' He turned to Michael's twin sister Millie, and said: 'I'm sorry I don't have a million pieces of paper for you Millie to write down *everything* you don't like about him.' He later explained that he considered Millie mature enough to take this kind of joke.

As if this wasn't humiliating enough, the head teacher then gathered up the pieces of paper and sat down with Michael outside of the classroom to go through the comments. It was nothing less than bullying in my book, and when I challenged the head teacher the next day, he tried to explain the exercise as a "Peer Review".

I was horrified, asked for a meeting at the school immediately – after which, the head wrote a four-page letter covering his back. In it, he mentioned that "he had experience in writing a document on ADHD – not that I am saying that Michael has it." ADHD or not, this was nothing short of head teacher-sanctioned bullying, and it had an immediate and devastating effect on Michael's friendships in the class. Sure enough in the playground the next day, Michael was the only boy left out of the football team in his class, and after the weekend, he suddenly didn't want to go back to school.

I spoke to the Head of Behaviour Policy at the council, who told me that the "Peer Review" the head teacher had quoted was only used for adults, and that 'Even for adults, only one negative is ever mentioned, which has to be balanced by at least five positive comments.' I contacted twin specialists, who advised me to separate the twins by sending them to different schools at this stage. I spoke to the educational counsellor, who had assessed Michael's IQ at age seven, and who was often used as an expert witness in cases involving breaches of school policy. He told me frankly that if you take on a head teacher, you take on a whole school – and the establishment will close rank.

In the end, I settled for resigning my governorship at the school, and visited another school in town, speaking at length to the head teacher about what had happened. He was sympathetic and offered Michael a place in the classroom with a promise that the special needs teacher would do some work with Michael around the incident. Within two weeks, mid-October, he moved into yet another school in the local town of East Grinstead.

MOVE IN DIFFERENT DIRECTIONS

Now I had three children in three different schools all with similar drop-off and pick-up times. I had burnt my bridges with a couple of parents, through forgetting to pick up their offspring or being late or upsetting them by the article (see page 129), and I was finding it hard to juggle. My husband was in London all day, and I had no childcare. That is when I made the fateful mistake of putting Michael, a primary school boy, on the secondary school bus – a mistake that led to him being knocked down by a car overtaking it one morning.

Impulsively, he had got off the bus, and run across the road, after the bus driver announced a different route for Sports Day that morning. As he ran across, a car was overtaking the stationery bus – and knocked him down, breaking his leg in two places and causing concussion where he hit the ground. I was called back from my walk to the shop, after dropping him at the bus stop, to find him in a pool of blood in the road. He was ten years old when he took his first helicopter ride, in a clingfilm cocoon, with me riding next to him in the air ambulance. It would be a further two years until he received his diagnosis, with me trying to understand during that time why so much drama and bad luck seemed to be dogging his early schooldays. We were a family in crisis during that period. My own ADHD was blocking my ability to see his, and perhaps, for the first time, "moving" was no longer an option. We were stuck, and needed help to move on.

PROFILE OF ANDREA BILBOW OBE

Andrea Bilbow is president of ADHD Europe and founder of ADDISS (ADD Information and Support Service).

It's a tribute to the resilience and stamina of Andrea Bilbow that after twenty-five years of advocacy and support for parents dealing with ADHD children in the UK, she still feels that the last two years have been among the best. A project, local to the headquarters for ADDISS in Barnet, London, offered intensive, wraparound support to 200 ADHD families locally with psychoeducation, courses in behaviour management, and weekly support, including training for teachers. The results were "way better than expected. It stopped at the end of August 2019, and we were predicted a 10% shift in outcomes, and we achieved double that with 20%. Families were telling us that it had literally saved their lives," says Bilbow, who was given an OBE in recognition of her work. She hopes the same model might be taken up by the borough of Haringey.

All this is very impressive for a woman who has ADHD herself, was diagnosed in her thirties following her two sons' diagnoses, one of whom is now married with a child, and the other who is living independently with a co-existing condition of Asperger's Syndrome. Despite having all of this on her plate, she was still driven to start a support group in her living room some twenty-five years ago because "there was absolutely no information anywhere about attention deficit".

Bilbow went from her living room to travel the world and meet ADHD professionals, attending her first American CHADD (Children and Adults with Attention Deficit Hyperactivity Disorder) conference in Washington DC in 1995, which inspired her to organise a similar conference in the UK. The resulting three-day international conference in the UK has become the most important event to educate parents and practitioners in the country. Now she is also president of ADHD Europe, where she is forging closer links with European countries, some of whom like Sweden and Denmark are further ahead than the UK in offering good care.

In the UK, she still feels that there is much work to be done: *I have seen us going backwards in some respects recently, as we lose good clinicians who educate themselves around ADHD, being replaced by jobbing psychiatrists with a one-size-fits all approach to medication. You can't just read about ADHD in a book – you have to have proper training, talk and listen to patients to learn about it.* It is this kind of plain speaking that brings real help to parents who need the advocacy to get the right treatment for their children.

CALL TO ACTION

This restlessness, translated in later life as an urge to move on – whether by moving house, area, school, job is now something I recognise and am able to tackle in different ways. Instead of moving house, again, I now think how can I add to my existing living space/job to make it new or more exciting? This year, during lockdown, I added three chickens and a chicken run to our garden, and volunteered by setting up four food collection points locally, getting funding from the local charity I worked with for the teenage mothers to add recipe cards and ingredient bags for a council emergency food bank. I also set up a podcast on Spotify (*The ADHD Lockdown Diaries*) with positive news stories. The trick is to channel that restless energy into something productive. Restlessness, if recognised, can be another superpower.

CHAPTER 14
MONEY AND THE LAW

"ADHD is associated with significant financial and emotional costs to the healthcare system, education services, carers and families, and society as a whole. Providing effective treatment will improve the quality of life of individuals with ADHD, their carers and their families, and at the same time will reduce the financial implications and psychological burden of ADHD to society."

The NICE guideline on diagnosis and management of ADHD in children, young people and adults, 2018

As well as writing for *The Times,* I also wrote for a number of property and financial magazines, on managing money, balancing credit cards and the like. Ironic, when piling up in the corner were my own mountain of receipts awaiting for the two-week horror of tackling my annual accounts.

As mentioned earlier, Thomas E Brown, author of a number of books on ADHD, and a Yale professor, argues that "situational variability is to do with interest and emotion, and that these two aspects help mask the usual problems with the 'executive function' part of the brain to do with planning and organisation, and working memory." So, if you are interested in something, you can override the procrastination of getting down to do it. Says Brown: "The motivating power of such 'interest' may be most apparent when it is absent, as described in the chronic complaints of many adults with ADHD who report that although they can 'hyperfocus' on activities in which they have special interest, they chronically find themselves unable to mobilise effort for tasks in which they do not feel any special immediate interest, *even when they are fully aware that their failure to do that uninteresting task may cause significant problems later*".[79] [my italics]. Procrastination is a terrible master. The best part about stimulant medication is it allows you to tackle that pile of receipts with the calm focus of a Jedi master. Imagine how much anxiety it causes when you know you need to do something, but still cannot get down to doing it?

Being freelance, and having to organise my finances, keep receipts, and most importantly file tax returns presented a new challenge. One thing I knew from my experience of running *RASP* magazine and a limited company was that I had little interest in figures. I had the energy and determination to run a company, but VAT returns, forms for Companies' House, and the constraints of filling in small boxes in an accounting ledger never struck me as urgent.

Likewise, any money I ever received for freelance journalism, which is not well-paid without regular columns, was spent before it arrived in my account. I always managed, but I was pretty hopeless at keeping hold of money. Good at spending it though.

So, when I attended the international ADHD conference in Liverpool in 2013, and saw a lecture on ADHD and financial mismanagement, I laughed. What on earth did they have to do with each other, I wondered? It was only when I got home and opened a bill from the Inland Revenue for a penalty of £1,400, due to a late filing of my tax return, that the penny dropped, as it were. Whether it's the lack of planning, the distractibility, procrastination, or the impulsive spending – there can be a real cost to this disorder. For example, forgetting to register my car to a new address (having

79 Brown, T.E., *Attention-Deficit Disorders and Comorbidities in Children, Adolescents and Adults*, 1st edn (Arlington, VA: American Psychiatric Publishing Inc: 2000) p18.

moved house again) and then forgetting to pay a £6 bill for crossing a bridge, escalated the Dartford Tunnel charge to £600, while the mounting penalties escalated on the doormat of a house I had moved from. I rang up to protest, and was given a choice of a "strict liability offence of £1,000 for having the car registered at the wrong address" or the £600 for the fine. Caught between a rock and a hard place, I had no choice but to pay it.

As one study put it: *Adults who had ADHD in adolescence are more likely to have high financial stress in later life. One of the mechanisms that may play a key role in creating the circumstances for high financial stress is the lower level of income attained by adults with ADHD. However, even after controlling for income, ADHD is still related to financial stress. It may be that the distractibility associated with ADHD interferes with financial planning and maintaining control over one's financial resources. This is likely to contribute to anxiety regarding one's finances and economic future.*[80]

Why this is important to know is, if you know yourself, and you know your weaknesses, you can militate against them. Although expensive, after my diagnosis, I used accountants to hassle me to get my tax affairs back in order when freelance, even though I resented paying them. Despite their £1,000 fees, they usually ended up saving me more money than they cost me. While the whole tax system was geared to people like me doing it ourselves online, I chose not to fail repeatedly to meet the 31 January deadline (the earlier October one being a joke), but to farm out my shortcomings. What a liberation. They also carried forward debts so I miraculously didn't pay some years, so the accountants were worth their fees in their clever accounting. For me, diagnosis has been as much about letting go of the things that I thought I *should* be able to do, but wasn't getting around to doing, and taking up more of the things that I actually enjoy doing, like staging theatre productions in the school holidays.

---

80 Brook, J.S., Brook, D.W., Zhang, C, Seltzer, N, & Finch, S.J., 'Adolescent ADHD and adult physical and mental health, work performance, and financial stress', *Pediatrics*, *131*(1), p.10.

I did eventually submit my accounts and appeal against the Inland Revenue for the £1,400 late payment fine (it was the first year the Inland Revenue had introduced it, and it climbed at £10 a day after the deadline, hence its size). I decided to mention in my covering letter my recent diagnosis of ADHD as part of the explanation, as much out of interest really, expecting the usual formal refusal of any extenuating circumstances. So, imagine my surprise when they cancelled the penalty, with no explanation. I am not saying the ADHD swung it, nor am I expecting special measures or "extra time" for those with my kind of disorder – but, all the same, I punched the air. One small victory for the neuroatypicals. Perhaps there was some small recognition of the challenges of the neurodiverse. Thank you, Mr Tax Man. Not a sentence I thought I would ever write.

HOW TO UNDERSTAND ADHD IN RELATION TO THE EQUALITY ACT 2010

Another reason why "Knowing is Better", as the 2016 ADHD Awareness Week slogan went, is because ADHD is actually classified as a disability in the law, and those with a diagnosis are protected by the Equality Act 2010. This means in the UK there is a law that bans unfair treatment of those with ADHD and helps to achieve equal opportunities in the workplace, schools, and in wider society.

The Equality Act defines disability as a "physical *or mental* impairment that has a substantial and long-term adverse effect on the person's ability to carry out day to day duties" [my italics]. It goes on to set out the different ways in which it is unlawful to treat someone, such as direct and indirect discrimination, harassment, and failing to make a "reasonable adjustment" for a disabled person. The Act also prohibits unfair treatment in the workplace when providing goods, facilities, and services.

POSITIVE ACTION

Schools, workplaces, and public offices are allowed to treat disabled pupils/employees more favourably than non-disabled ones, and in some cases are required to do so, by making "reasonable adjustments" to put them on a more level footing with others who don't have a disability. This would probably be called "levelling up" in current talk. This treating of an ADHD person differently is also known in the law as "positive action".

Digging a little deeper, the law states that discrimination is unlawful behaviour in three different ways. First, direct discrimination, when one person treats another less favourably because of a protected characteristic – for example, if a teacher were to punish a student for an ADHD trait such as fidgeting, or impulsive calling out.

Secondly, there is indirect discrimination, when a "practice" is applied across a group and puts people with a particular characteristic at a disadvantage. And, finally, there is harassment or "unwanted conduct, related to a relevant protected characteristic which has the purpose or effect of violating a person's dignity or creating an intimidating, hostile, degrading, humiliating or offensive environment for that person." This covers any unpleasant and bullying behaviour.

LEGAL ACTION

The Equalities Act 2010 does not offer any more protection for those with ADHD, but does set out a bit more clearly the responsibility of schools and workplaces to ensure those with a diagnosis have the same opportunities as their non-disabled peers. Parents have used the Act when pupils have been excluded for behavioural issues, for example, such as the case of Grace, excluded for answering back, and refusing to follow instructions over a uniform infringement[81]. After the case went to tribunal in

[81] Entecott, L, 'Challenging Disability Discrimination', *ADHD News*, Issue 18, Spring 2012.

the UK, Grace's parents won their case against the school, and the staff at the school were ordered to have training in ADHD as a result. It was a landmark case for those with ADHD in the UK, and the first time that the disorder was recognised in the law in this way. I hope that it might encourage parents of children who are suspended, as happened to my ADHD son, before he started medication, to also push back against schools. It would really help to raise awareness of the condition – something that I see as shockingly poorly understood in schools, even in 2020.

ADHD AWARENESS

Because of my own late diagnosis, and my subsequent decision to go into teaching modern foreign languages in secondary schools – I am "out" about my ADHD. I consider myself an advocate of the condition, and if the state education system in the UK can't handle an employee who has ADHD, who can? This means I raise it in the initial job interview, and there is usually a short discussion where the school asks all the right questions: 'What does this mean? Do you need any additional support?'

My reply is: 'Just a ring-fence around my weekly coaching [therapy] sessions, which support me.' I am not asking them to agree to something that happens within school hours, but in teaching, once the term starts, it's amazing how the workload begins to creep up and before you know it, there are parents' evenings, departmental meetings, Continued Professional Development sessions, and after-school detentions that demand that "one hour a week".

I negotiate my weekly coaching session before I start at a school, and keep it sacred. As 40% of Newly Qualified Teachers (NQTs) leave within the first five years of teaching, I know that this session could mean the difference between becoming a martyr to the educational cause, or maintaining enough boundaries to last the course. It's also a necessary safe place to sound off, given that my lowly status as a Newly Qualified Teacher means that I have to shut up and put up most of the time.

REASONABLE ADJUSTMENTS

When I started teaching in my current school, I was not given a classroom but was timetabled to teach in thirteen different teachers' classrooms. As a result, I began to lose things along the way, and the effort to keep hold of my teaching resources as well as to arrive at the next lesson with all my books and equipment in hand, quickly became overwhelming. Most of the teachers understood the difficulty of teaching in other people's classrooms, and agreed it was challenging (even without ADHD), so I knew that I was not complaining without good reason. I sat with a person in Human Resources to ask whether I could be given a classroom as a reasonable adjustment for my ADHD. My newly appointed Head of Department offered me hers, as a result, and I agreed to take it.

In the end, the senior leadership team didn't allow it, but if I had decided to stay longer at the school, I could have insisted on my own classroom. The fact that the legal framework was there in place to make me feel confident about asking for help was an important first step in making the request, and I would have been quite within my rights to demand some positive action legally as well. It is diagnosis that gives you this confidence to ask for more help to make the playing field level, and wherever I eventually end up working, I will make sure this principle is honored.

THE DEFINITION OF A DISABILITY

Below is an extract from the 2010 Equality Act, which shows the level of detail the law considers when determining which traits of ADHD qualify.

A young man has Attention Deficit Hyperactivity Disorder (ADHD) which manifests itself in a number of ways, including exhibitionism and an inability to concentrate. The disorder, as an impairment which has a substantial and long-term adverse effect on the young person's ability to carry out normal day-to-day activities, would be a disability for the purposes of the Act.

The young man is not entitled to the protection of the Act in relation to any discrimination he experiences as a consequence of his exhibitionism, because that is an excluded condition under the Act.

However, he would be protected in relation to any discrimination that he experiences in relation to the non-excluded effects of his condition, such as inability to concentrate. For example, he would be entitled to any reasonable adjustments that are required as a consequence of those effects.

(Extract from the Office for Disability issues, HM Government. Equality Act 2010. Guidance on matters taken into account when determining issues relating to the definition of a disability.)[82]

CALL TO ACTION

If you could wave your magic wand and ask one thing of your workplace, what would it be? What would be the "reasonable adjustment" you might crave for yourself or a member of your family or friend to help them really thrive in their current environment? If you were to know that this concept is enshrined in law, would that embolden you to ask for it? It helped me as a newly qualified teacher, and while it didn't increase my pay packet, having the knowledge that it underpinned my rights within a working environment made me reflect on what I needed to thrive.

[82] UK Government, *Equality Act 2010*, 2015 <https://www.gov.uk/guidance/equality-act-2010-guidance> [accessed October 2018].

PART 3
THRIVE

CHAPTER 15
THERAPY

"I strongly urge my professional readers to continue advocating for the important role of including psychotherapy in the treatment of ADHD across the lifespan."

Dr Sam Goldstein, neuropsychologist and author[83]

Psychotherapist Sari Solden writes: *Even though each woman is different, there are some common themes among women seeking counselling for ADHD. The effects of living for a long time with undiagnosed ADHD include a distorted self-image, the pain of underachievement despite strengths and talents, and difficulty with mood or relationships … Overwhelmed by daily life, these women often become isolated, depressed, and ashamed of their perceived failings.* Therapy can help change all that. Through investment in this relationship, you can rebuild a more realistic view of yourself, do away with the shame of not feeling good enough, and rebuild new relationships and your life. Alain de Botton writes in the *School of Life: We aren't ever done with the odd business of becoming that most extraordinary and prized of things, an emotionally mature person, or, to put it a simpler way, an almost grown-up adult.*[84] Having someone at your side, who also has your back, to help you on that path of progress is an investment I've never regretted.

---

[83] Goldstein, S, *The role of psychotherapy in the Treatment of ADHD through the lifespan*, 2013 <https://ldaamerica.org/info/the-role-of-psychotherapy-in-the-treatment- of-adhd-through-the-lifespan/> [accessed: 8 August 2018].

[84] de Botton, A, *School of Life* (London: Penguin Random House, 2019), p.35.

Before starting therapy, I had done a number of courses that work on the basis of inducing a near-spiritual high in the participants, often through the sharing of some secret that has burdened people throughout their life. As a journalist, I was a trained observer on the outside, so I found my natural sceptisicm hard to put to one side to engage. The courses, such as Outlook, Essence, and the Experience, helped me to open up more, to approach strangers on the street knowing that we all carry a burden of some sort in our heart, but, whatever it was I was after in those rooms was not going to be fixed in the space of a week's self-development course.

By my early thirties, there was something else going on that I was obviously unaware of; an inability to settle down and get on with life, in the way that many of my friends were now beginning to do. On the outside, everything was looking good. My husband Adam and I had a flat in London, we had a baby, and we were both getting our careers together – Adam as a lawyer in the music business and me as a journalist at *The Times*. So why then did I feel so overwhelmed by juggling it all, particularly the relationship and a baby? We had always had explosive rows, and I had even left Adam for a short while with our son tucked under my arm to spend a few weeks outside London with a divorced friend, running away from it all. There in her cramped house, the hard work and reality of single parenthood struck me, as she coped valiantly on her own with two toddlers. I slunk back home to tackle the problems head on.

This was the point at which I dragged Adam off to couple therapy, where we bonded over disliking the intensely annoying therapist, so were able to agree on at least one thing. While that helped us to set aside our differences, the restlessness continued, and I insisted that at least one of us should be in therapy to tackle our endless domestic rows. Adam refused to go, so then I – reluctantly – agreed. Perhaps because of the courses I had already done, I felt I had dragged myself through the self-development process enough, and had heard so many stories from those who had suffered abuse, that I felt the problem must lie with

Adam and not me. This was my default defence tactic in most situations – I would lay the blame squarely at the feet of someone else. If the courses had proved to be an interesting distraction, therapy was to be a liberating form of support.

THERAPEUTIC RELATIONSHIP

Although I found the relationship with a therapist worse than awkward to begin with, therapy was immediately helpful. I realised that the group work I'd done on the courses was not what I really needed; what worked better for me was the lack of distraction that came with two chairs and a room where I wasn't going to be interrupted for fifty minutes. My therapist was a woman who had a strong French accent. I found her through a recommendation of a school called the Psychosynthesis and Education Trust. She answered the phone when I rang up to enquire, sounded suitably sympathetic, and pretty soon I found myself trekking off weekly to see her.

Alain de Botton writes: *Part of what therapy offers us is a chance to improve how we judge ourselves and the voices we hear in our heads. It can involve learning – in a conscious, deliberate way – to speak to ourselves in the manner the therapist once spoke to us over many months.*[85] Almost immediately, I felt validated by someone who listened without judgement as I emptied my emotional handbag on the floor every week. Up until starting therapy, I had never shared my internal chattering with any stranger, and had a fairly rigid mask of competency that I would only let slip with friends. The demands of early motherhood, a career, and a husband were now leaving me less time for my usual support network of friends, and I felt trapped by the impossibility of making it all work. Like an overloaded system, I felt in danger of blowing a gasket and ruining my marriage.

Says Alain de Botton: *An inner voice was always an outer voice that we have – imperceptibly – made our own. We've absorbed the tone of a kind and gentle caregiver who liked to laugh indulgently at our foibles and had*

---

[85] Ibid.

endearing names for us. Or else we have taken in the voice of a harassed or angry person, never satisfied with anything we achieved and full of rage and contempt.[86] Now I am not saying that a lot of women with ADHD are not blessed with kind parents, but with all the challenges that accompany ADHD, and the well-documented studies showing how much more likely they are to suffer some form of abuse by parents[87], it is unsurprising that we have a negative inner critic. Like the behaviour specialist who explained why the "Peer Review" strategy employed by that head teacher was so wrong (see page 153); if you give children a lot of negative feedback, they only hear that – not the positive comments. People with ADHD need to hear the "good enough" message repeatedly to offset the years of hearing the opposite in a neurotypical world.

ADHD was never in the picture when I started my therapy in 2001 – it would be another seven years before Adult ADHD even existed in the UK as a diagnosis. What had started as an attempt to show Adam how serious I was about making the relationship work, then turned into a way of keeping me on track, as I then fell pregnant with twins and felt I needed more support.

While I hope the next generation won't think twice about taking themselves off to see a shrink when problems arise, for my generation there was always a furtive, slightly shameful feeling around needing it. Back then, I was conscious that I might bump into someone I knew en route to the therapist, and have to explain what was I doing in Balham at this hour, and where exactly I was going. On one visit to my therapist, I bumped into a friend of my sister-in-law who lived right across the street, and after that I would always put my collar up as I left for the car, for fear of meeting her.

For my parents' generation, therapy was even more shameful, considered as a last-ditch attempt to hang on to your sanity before being committed to an asylum. Until recently my mother was mistrustful about the necessity of the process and didn't like me

---

86 Ibid., p.57

87 Briscoe-Smith, A.M., Hinshaw, S.P., 'Linkages between child abuse and attention-deficit/hyperactivity disorder in girls: behavioral and social correlates', *Child abuse & neglect*, *30*(11), pp.1239–1255.

going at all. 'What *do* you talk about?' she used to ask. 'No doubt you have a good old moan about me,' she worried.

Without therapy along the way though, I doubt I would still be married, or have a good relationship with my children. Therapy has literally been like the stabilisers on my bicycle (that I have still to get rid of). With all my anger and my explosive nature, I was often storming out of rooms and relationships, and then not knowing quite how to tiptoe back in. Therapy offered me a relationship that I wasn't able to bugger up, somewhere to rehearse my comeback speech for that week or to manage issues with a boss. Also, I wasn't used to exploring my feelings; up until therapy, action rather than reflection was my way of being in the world.

THERAPIST AS ADVOCATE

Perhaps most importantly, the therapist was on my side. She was my champion, and could offer me a different perspective. I always seemed to leave the room feeling lighter than when I walked in. With my first therapist, we did a lot of "chair" work, where I would talk to the problem person in the chair, and then be the problem person giving the answer. Exploring both sides of a problem this way was quite revolutionary for someone as bull-headed as myself. Not only did this help me to see both sides of the issues in, say, my marriage, but also it helped me to understand how working on my reaction to a situation meant I could change it. I quickly understood that there is no point being right in a relationship, if being right means continual conflict (not that I was usually right, I just *thought* I was).

However, a lifetime of making mistakes had made me sensitive to being called out about it. I used to become aggressive when challenged, and it took me a long time to get over minding being "wrong" when caught out. Plus, I had been attracted to an opposite in my husband. He is a lawyer, used to putting the finer detail in place, and he *hated* getting anything wrong. Part of having things in their natural order means he likes to tidy up as soon as he gets in from work, for example, and I was struggling with how his insistence on coming home to a clear space was making me feel inadequate as a home-maker. So what if the place was a bit messy? What did he expect with three small kids?

Add to this my military upbringing, and the legacy of being sent to boarding school aged ten, and often it seemed that the only emotion I could access easily was anger. My mother had always hated sadness and tears, so we were not a family that were allowed to wallow, and being told to "cheer up" was her way of dealing with difficult emotions. I could do the class clown easily enough, make others laugh, or make a joke out of a situation, but sadness, seriousness, grief, and tears were an entirely unfamiliar language in our household. One of my favourite lines in Lara Honos-Webb's book *The Gift of Adult ADHD*[88] is where she describes all ADHDers as "recovering class clowns".

Therapists see through the class-clown shtick fast. They tend to have a box of tissues somewhere in the room for their clients for tears of sadness, not of laughter. Indeed, my therapist would find herself flustered when I made her laugh – or when I laughed, which was my default mode when telling some detail about a difficult day or a troublesome colleague. 'But why are you laffing when you are telling me zis terrible story?' she would ask, fighting back laughter herself, trying to find her balance again.

In therapy speak, I suppose my therapist represented a "Good Enough Mother" figure – she was comfortable with melancholy, and wasn't driven by the need to stay cheerful at all costs like my own mother. For the war generation, keeping your chin up came as naturally as the phrase "mustn't grumble" and "keep the home fires burning" – and we were raised in the "cheer up, love, it may never happen" era of emotional intelligence.

THERAPY ABUSE

The therapeutic relationship can be enormously helpful, but it comes with a lot of responsibility, and it is vital to find someone

[88] Honos-Webb L, *The Gift of Adult ADD: How to Transform Your Challenges and Build on Your Strengths* (Sydney: Accessible Publishing Systems, 2008), p.244.

accredited, part of a recognised organisation, and supervised. Until relatively recently in the UK, psychotherapy was woefully unregulated, and anyone could set themselves up as a counsellor or life coach if they wanted. I had a friend who was unsupervised and unqualified, as well as being extremely charismatic, who led some meditation courses and offered to take me on as a client.

I should have known better, because she claimed to have a direct connection to God, and instead of ringing alarm bells, it made her difficult to challenge. I stupidly agreed to be counselled by her, and it was to be a damaging experience, that ended badly after a couple of years when she accused me of causing her to fall and hurt herself in her own flat, while I was miles away. She was losing the plot somewhat, and I didn't know then as I do now that you cannot mix friendship and therapy. I wasn't sufficiently aware of why this wasn't a healthy relationship, and looking back on it, I see it as a form of emotional abuse.

Undiagnosed, and aware how helpful therapy had been in the past, I was perhaps more vulnerable than a normally wired person to being preyed upon by someone like this. It wasn't just that I was easily led, but I was too eager for answers from someone who insisted that she spoke the truth and had access to some higher divine power. I found her certainty attractive, sitting alongside my own lack of sureness as a mother, although I know now that being directed in a certain way is the opposite of therapy.

It took work with a third registered and supervised therapist to point out how very wrong this so-called "friendship" was. By that point, I had made a couple of life decisions with the friend-come-therapist's encouragement, including moving out of London to be nearer to where she lived, and recruiting others to sign up to her sessions. While I don't believe the friend/therapist's intentions were malicious, it was just too easy for her to point out my failures, to be too involved in my marriage, and to give advice on my children, when the reality was that she should not have been practising.

Therapy is a powerful tool, because of the power someone can wield over you. It should be very boundaried, be about offering a safe space to explore your own path and not to be told a better way. Being listened to on a deep level is a transformational experience. Being told what to do by someone who wants to fix you is just plain wrong.

COACHING FOR LIFE

When requalifiying as a teacher after my diagnosis, I renamed the therapy that I still have regularly as "coaching" and it became part of my "learning support plan": one hour in the week outside of school that couldn't be moved. A lifetime of ADHD takes its toll, and going back into school was always going to be difficult for me, having had such a difficult time there as a teenager. Ironically, the very difficulty seemed to have helped me to develop a healthy resilience to the slings and arrows of the teaching world, and the intense compressed experience of teacher training. When the exhaustion that drives many to the edge triggered moments of despair, I always had the balm of the counselling session to smooth things over. Because I have had a champion of a therapist at my side throughout, I have been able to use many of those ADHD traits, such as energy and resilience, to my advantage.

I believe that it is part of the complexity of the condition that when you feel emotionally held, encouraged, and made to feel powerful, you feel you can tackle any challenge thrown at you. During my diagnosis, the ADHD psychiatrist said that I had obviously had so many years of therapy because therapy "couldn't fix what was wrong". In my mind, he wasn't entirely right. I had had so many years of therapy not because I felt like I needed fixing, but because therapy was so helpful.

TEN THINGS YOU SHOULD KNOW BEFORE ENGAGING WITH THERAPY

1) In the UK, therapists should be registered with the BACP – British Association of Counselling and Practitioners – or another professional body that is recognised and accredited in other countries.
2) According to the BACP Code of Ethics introduced in 2018, supervision is essential to how practitioners sustain good practice throughout their working life. Check any therapist you work with has regular supervision.
3) Life coaches offer a different service to therapists; they tend to focus on the practical, rather than the emotional, aspects of support for ADHD. Largely unregulated by professional bodies, you would need to check out the reviews and qualifications for a life coach.
4) Make sure you have an idea of what you want to get out of therapy, and agree a number of sessions at the start. This can be reviewed as you near that number. If you leave it open-ended, therapy can be hard to stop once you start.
5) There are many different types of therapy from Freudian and Kleinian psychoanalysis, to Gestalt, Humanist, Psychodynamic, Integrative, and Cognitive Behavioural Therapy (CBT). Any therapist subscribing to one model should be on the website of that particular branch of therapy, i.e. in the UK, the accredited therapists specialising in Gestalt Therapy will be on the main Gestalt website (www.gestaltcentre.org). Make sure you read their profile before signing up.

6) Choosing a therapist is not only about finding the right person. Often matters such as how accessible they are, whether you can reach them easily by transport are just as important. There are many ways to choose a therapist, but choosing one that is local and offers a type of therapy that chimes with your values and needs is a good way to start.
7) The therapeutic "hour" usually lasts for fifty minutes, and costs anything from £50 upwards. Most therapists expect you to engage weekly for a certain amount of sessions, so check that you can afford it before beginning.
8) The difference between a psychiatrist and a psychotherapist or counsellor is that psychiatrist is trained as a medical doctor in the area of psychiatry, the study of mental health. The latter two are trained to help people overcome troublesome habits and emotional problems.
9) In the UK, the NHS does offer therapy, but the waiting lists are long and it is hard to come by. The main form of therapy offered is CBT (Cognitive Behavioural Therapy) for anxiety, depression, OCD, and phobias. Anxiety and depression are the most common comorbidities with ADHD, so some help may be available free of charge.
10) Always ask for a trial period. If you don't feel the therapy is working after the first or second session, or you don't gel with the therapist, try someone else. It takes time to build a relationship, but trust your instincts if you are not making progress and feeling better about yourself early on.

PROFILE OF JOYCE BLAKE, COGNITIVE BEHAVIOURAL THERAPIST

Cognitive Behavioural Therapy (CBT) is recommended in the NICE Guidelines[89] as the talking therapy that has the best evidence base for the treatment of individuals with ADHD and their unhelpful habits and behaviours. There are many therapists who promote themselves as "CBT trained", but this could simply mean that they attended a weekend workshop. So, if you are interested in finding an accredited CBT practitioner privately in the UK, it is best to visit the British Association for Behavioural and Cognitive Psychotherapies (BABCP) www.babcp.com.

Joyce Blake works with clients who have ADHD in the NHS and in private practice, and gives some idea below of what help clients may expect from treatment:

CBT is a short-term, collaborative, and goal-orientated form of therapy that focuses on the way that our thoughts, feelings, physical sensations, and behaviours are all connected. This can be especially important for people with ADHD, who may have experienced a lifetime of making mistakes and missing deadlines, which has led to them feeling more self-critical and having lower self-esteem. Indeed, it is common for individuals with ADHD to also experience depression, anxiety, and/or substance use issues.

A typical course of CBT for clients with ADHD is likely to comprise of strategies to help them improve their organisation and planning; learn key skills to manage their distractibility, and gain insight into the ways that their unhelpful thinking styles, which are common to all people, may be hindering them and creating a vicious

89 National Institute of Clinical Excellence provides guidelines for the NHS on best practice. The guidelines on ADHD diagnosis and management updated in 2018 can be found here: <https://www.nice.org.uk/guidance/ng87/chapter/Recommendations#diagnosis>

cycle of difficulties. The primary aim is to give the client effective coping strategies for issues that impact on their everyday life, rather than addressing the core symptoms of hyperactivity and impulsivity. Treatment usually comprises of around twelve (fifty-minute) weekly sessions, sometimes less on the NHS, but this can, of course, be reviewed by both parties.

Common issues for people with ADHD are difficulties with procrastination and time-management when the task appears overwhelming. CBT can help the client learn skills to break the task down into smaller parts. Many clients report that they don't get on with tasks because they get distracted by other, less important things getting in the way. CBT can also help with strategies to help overcome this type of behaviour.

One of the key aims of CBT is to challenge the individual's negative beliefs (e.g. "I am not good enough" or "I will fail") and to learn to deal with their difficulties in a more positive way. These negative beliefs will be explored in therapy to help challenge and break any unhelpful cycles (e.g. "there is no point in even trying as I will just mess up again") that may be blocking the client from reaching their full potential.

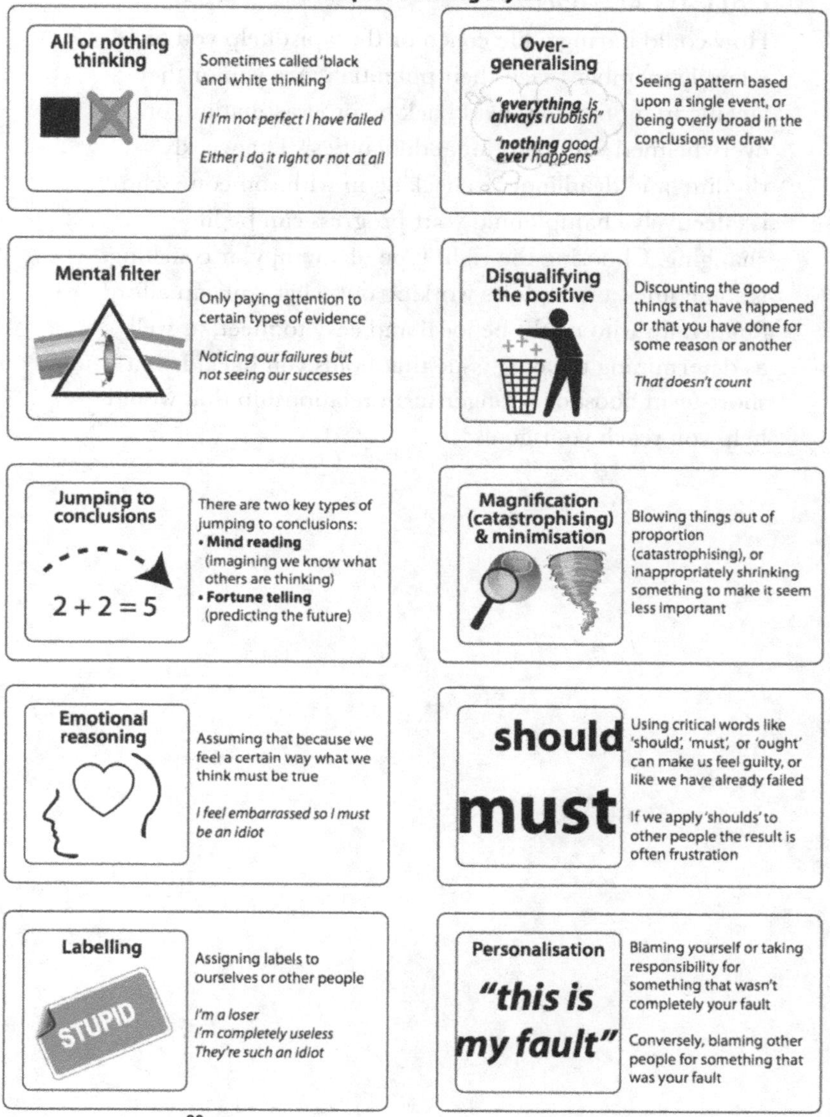
Unhelpful Thinking Styles

All or nothing thinking
Sometimes called 'black and white thinking'
If I'm not perfect I have failed
Either I do it right or not at all

Over-generalising
"everything is always rubbish"
"nothing good ever happens"
Seeing a pattern based upon a single event, or being overly broad in the conclusions we draw

Mental filter
Only paying attention to certain types of evidence
Noticing our failures but not seeing our successes

Disqualifying the positive
Discounting the good things that have happened or that you have done for some reason or another
That doesn't count

Jumping to conclusions
2 + 2 = 5
There are two key types of jumping to conclusions:
- **Mind reading** (imagining we know what others are thinking)
- **Fortune telling** (predicting the future)

Magnification (catastrophising) & minimisation
Blowing things out of proportion (catastrophising), or inappropriately shrinking something to make it seem less important

Emotional reasoning
Assuming that because we feel a certain way what we think must be true
I feel embarrassed so I must be an idiot

should
must
Using critical words like 'should', 'must', or 'ought' can make us feel guilty, or like we have already failed
If we apply 'shoulds' to other people the result is often frustration

Labelling
STUPID
Assigning labels to ourselves or other people
I'm a loser
I'm completely useless
They're such an idiot

Personalisation
"this is my fault"
Blaming yourself or taking responsibility for something that wasn't completely your fault
Conversely, blaming other people for something that was your fault

PSYCHOLOGYTOOLS[90]

[90] Figure: 1 *'Unhelpful Thinking Styles'* (Psychology Tools, 2018)

CALL TO ACTION

How could having a life coach or therapist help you or a family member reach their potential? Are you or they lacking in motivation, held back by procrastination, or overwhelmed with emotional difficulties? The weekly rhythm (and deadline) of checking in with someone who is effectively championing your progress can be life-changing. Choosing the right type of therapy or coaching is sometimes as simple as working out what you can afford financially, who might be local and easy to meet, as well as determining the core issue that holds you back. Is it a short-term boost or a longer-term relationship that would help you reach your goals?

CHAPTER 16
CELEBRATE ADHD

"A small part of me still believes that to be the person in the room with the most feelings is to be the best person. I know it's not wise or fashionable to say so, but it is one way of having maximum life."

Susie Boyt, in her last column for the *Financial Times*

Once the initial shock of diagnosis was over, I began to understand that while everything had changed, also nothing had changed. The only real difference was that I now had a clearer understanding of myself, and how my brain worked. I therefore could adapt, rather than improvise to overcome difficulties.

What I understood was that there was an upside to making a lot of mistakes all the time. It gave permission to people to be in the right, to show their kinder side, and usually gave me a chance to strike up a conversation with a stranger. Because I realised that I was versed in the ways of those in the wrong, I could relate to the wayward, the underdog, the disempowered, and the young. ADHD is human frailty and error writ large, and the kindness of strangers is always there, usually with the quip, 'Don't worry love, it could happen to anyone.' As we divide our lives into pre-Covid and post-Covid, everyone can now see this.

I also understood that too many people are afraid to make mistakes, or hate making them; so much so that they will go to extremes not to, or to cover them up, while I see making mistakes as part of life. In my worldview, it is far better to make your own mistakes than to be ensnared in a relationship with someone trying to correct you all the time, which has happened in the past. In fact, one of the best reasons why "knowing is better" is that it helped me to avoid all those kind of toxic friendships or relationships, the ones that dragged me down, because I appeared like a problem that needed to be fixed. Often the fixer types are frightened by adventure and not open to the spontaneous and new opportunities in life, so do they really deserve to be in charge?

THE BEST QUALITIES OF ADHD

The qualities of bigheartedness, fun, generosity, sensitivity, intuition, energy, creativity, frankness, and expressiveness don't necessarily tally with those of capitalism and the rat race, but many of the people I know who have ADHD have these qualities in spades. They are also brave, because they battle with their atypical brain in a typical-brained world every day, and have that kind of resilience that others can only dream of.

Give my son someone younger to help, such as a new-to-the-school younger buddy, and a new side to his personality emerges. In June each year Arseny, a young Russian boy from Belarus, comes to stays with us as part of a charity initiative called Friends of Chernobyl Children, and Michael turns into this caring, concerned older brother figure with seemingly endless time on his hands. It is Michael who bounces on the trampoline with him or jumps out at him from behind doors wearing a Halloween horror mask, and he is the one who carries Arseny up to bed on his back, plays water pistols in the garden, and takes over most of the burden of entertainment during his month in the UK.

Arseny first came over aged seven, as part of a group of twelve other Russian children funded by a charity dedicated to providing a holiday for kids living in a poor and contaminated area of Belarus, badly affected by the fallout from the Chernobyl nuclear disaster. The children return over four years to give them a holiday, and to improve their immune systems and get some health and dental checks. When Arseny first stayed, Michael formed the strongest bond with him immediately. He was the one who suddenly had the patience to show him how to play Lego. In an effective handout for teachers pioneered in 2009 by Tymms and Merrill called: "Tips for Managing Children with Severe Attentional Difficulties"[91], it specifically recommends: "Give the pupil with ADHD a younger student to coach." Such a simple and effective instruction, and a reminder of how education around this condition, where, say, all schools could easily introduce a positive mentor system to handle students with ADHD, and thereby benefit the wider school community, instead of punishing these disruptive kids with the current Victorian method of endless detentions.

I wonder why providing help to younger students is recommended from research, and why it brings out the best in children with severe attentional issues. Is it because those with ADHD recognise how grateful they are whenever someone shows them that kind of positive support? After all, none of us ever forget a good teacher, who "got" us, who encouraged us, and brought out the best – particularly if our schooldays weren't particularly happy ones.

I've spent a lot of my time as a mother taking my son's side, fighting with schools to get teachers and head teachers to see a different point of view, particularly before the diagnosis. In some senses, I was fighting my own battles with authority, second time around, trying to get them to see why stopping a child from doing PE because they were too boisterous walking down to the sports hall was the very opposite of what was needed as a punishment. Making them run around the pitch twice before starting PE is a far better idea, but please don't send them back to a classroom on their own.

After the acceptance of my own diagnosis, I was driven to revisit the one place that I vowed I would never return to – school. Teaching is called a vocation for a good reason – nobody

---

91 This was included by Professor Eric Taylor at his talk at 2016 ADDISS conference during ADHD awareness month in October.

persuades you to do it. All through your training, you have to hold on to your belief that this is important work as hurdle after hurdle is thrown in front of you, before you finally qualify. If you threaten to quit, or admit you are finding it too hard – no one tries to persuade you to stay. They know that you have to have the stamina to make it work, and only you can find that within you. My decision to change careers, a bolt from the blue, came while listening to Rabbi Jonathan Sacks on the BBC Radio 4 show *Thought for the Day*[92]. It was as if a lightning bolt had jumped out of the radio and given me an electric shock. I listened to the story of this new charity Now Teach, set up to help experienced professionals change careers – and I was hooked immediately.

Started by the *Financial Times* journalist Lucy Kellaway, and Katie Waldegrave, the charity aimed to help plug the current gap of 2,000 teachers currently lacking in the UK. "Having a high level of energy is one of the greatest gifts anyone can have; the older we get, the more obvious this becomes," says Lara Honos-Webb in the *Gift of Adult ADHD*, and this felt like an ideal place to put that energy.

I joined the "Now Teach" start-up and was part of the first cohort of older career changers, forty-seven assorted bankers, journalists, civil servants, foreign officer workers, and even a NASA scientist, as we all began this adventure of being at the very bottom of the ladder together. We were all determined not to be part of the statistics that show that 40% of trainee teachers leave in the first five years, and we knew from the outset that we would have each other as support.

Training to be a teacher is a lowly, humbling experience – you are thrown in to schools without much introduction, spend hours planning lessons, which are unlikely to work, and are humiliated by failing again and again. Initially it felt to me like you were given a piece of rope to hang yourself publicly, and not even told how to make the noose. However, a bit like the lockdown, we new

92 Sack, R, *The more you give, the more you'll be given*, 2016 <https://rabbisacks.org/working-young-helps-keep-young-thought-day/> [accessed March 2020].

teachers were all in it together, bonded by daily updates from a WhatsApp group where we could vent or share our trials and triumphs. Some of our first cohort were CEOs, who didn't even know how to work the photocopier because they had secretaries to do that for them, and miraculously all but a handful qualified that first year.

As we grew accustomed to the infantilising experience of being in school and having no status, most of us began to fathom how this could also be the most exciting job as well. When it works, circulating around the room and looking into pupils' exercise books to see that they *have* understood some grammar point you've just taught and are now demonstrating it in real time by making up sentences, or hearing a child communicate something in another language spontaneously after you have just taught them how, is both intoxicating and inexplicably thrilling.

The complexities of teaching are immense, not least because in our state-funded schools you are expected to differentiate with different work for the academically more able, and for those with special educational needs, and somehow get them all to behave as well. Also, the pace is frenetic. I had worked in four newsrooms for national newspapers, but nothing had prepared me for the speed needed to wave out one class of thirty pupils after a full hour of sweating through the subject, and then wave in another group lining up outside seconds later. While I needed to spend a whole day to plan lessons for the week, turning a five-day week into a six-day one, teaching immediately helped me to get better organised and manage my time more effectively. I spotted the obvious distracted and disruptive ADHDers in the room, and used to enjoy finding ways to keep their attention, or making them the messengers with paper registers, although I was continually surprised to find how very few of them had diagnoses. Without a diagnosis, they didn't technically qualify for additional support, and it was frustrating to see how many were slipping through the net.

I had gone into teaching with this ideal of helping a new generation, of giving something back and perhaps favouring those with special needs, but what I hadn't expected was how the challenge, routine, and timetable of the school would actually help *my* ADHD. Another benefit was that this was an environment where I could be open about my diagnosis, and I would explain that I take medication, which wears off at the end of the school day. It felt good to explain what the disorder meant as an adult to the school recruiting me, to advocate for it, and to propose how some of the traits leant themselves well to teaching, especially the energy needed. Most of the head teachers and deputy heads interviewing would ask what special concessions I needed.

I didn't find the career switch as difficult as many others in our first cohort, perhaps because I was used to finding things hard, despite having a really tough time during my training. Something switched in me during menopause, the relentless negativity of the news agenda, the drip feed of doom and gloom that engulfed me as I opened my newspaper daily had begun to wear me down. I could no longer read to the end of some stories of teenage stabbings on the street, the problems of the world began to feel personal and I had become more sensitive. After years of trying to "water the positive seeds" along Buddhist lines, through mindfulness training, perhaps some transformation had begun to take place.

With my diagnosis, I wanted to concentrate on something positive, to smile rather than frown, to channel that energy where it was needed. Good schools are like little castles of utopia, where drawbridges are drawn up as the gates clang close in the morning, and where sometimes the values might still be Victorian, but the politically correct language is utterly modern. You are taught to "catch them being good", "give them praise", "find positive targets" as you wield the red pen. Every educational establishment is founded on a wildly positive motto, even if they struggle to adhere to it.

Journalism needs scepticism, to doubt and prod the subject to find the truth, and I wanted something hopeful and benevolent, and working with children was just that. I had to park all my negativity outside the school gates before entering, or I couldn't get through the day. Plus, I had to promote a classroom culture where it is fine to make mistakes, that is how you learn, without shaming students – something that tapped into my own view of an imperfect world.

In three out of four of the schools where I worked, I set up lunchtime clubs – because I felt the state system lacked much fun or culture, particularly in modern languages. French and Russian clubs were to give pupils a weekly lunchtime activity to explore a bit of film or food from that region, or just to goof off and try talking in another language. I also set up Spanish food days with the catering staff in one school, and took one class of twelve-year-olds on a trip to the French Institute in London for a three-course meal including oysters (that part I shelled out for) and a French movie. The clubs, which were seen as somewhat eccentric by the other teachers, gave me ownership of something I could create in school, while still trying to crack the teacher training.

And all this is because my experience of ADHD is not as a deficit disorder, but as an abundance disorder. I asked the question after my diagnosis where does the ADHD start and my personality begin? I now see that the two are inextricably linked. We are formed by our parents, our upbringing, our environment, but there is always that streak of your own personality pushing through all of that to forge your own path. In the past, it might have been described as destiny, fate, or good luck, but I see it as the tiny choices you make all the time to create your own reality. The more I learn about ADHD, the more I see that it can be a useful genetic difference, and one that may well have a genetic benefit for the whole group or society we live in.

While some might link the genetic variation back to when hunters became farmers, or argue that it is part of a so-called "explorer" gene, 7R, I believe it continues down the line of the population, generation after generation, for a good reason. As one study maintains: *At a practical level, how could the children in a village benefit from having one or two children with ADHD–Hyperactive/Impulsive*

(HI) in their midst? The children with ADHD–HI do things they should not. They burn their hands on the stove. They eat poisonous berries and fall out of trees. They do not focus on their classwork, and they break the rules in games. All these physical and social mistakes provide useful lessons for the majority, while the majority remain safe. Much less often, but possibly also importantly, children with ADHD–HI discover something advantageous, that the other children would not.

In the modern world, without that impulsive, restless, distractible need for adventure, there would be far fewer companies set up, products launched, music and art created, and new solutions to old problems mooted. Diversity drives evolution, and neurodiversity needs acceptance to be tolerated and celebrated properly.

A BETTER FUTURE

Remembering that ADHD can cause a great deal of harm to those who have it, as well as having a social cost, if undiagnosed, untreated, and misunderstood, the stigma around naming or labelling it has to be faced head on. Just one generation ago, left-handed students in school were forced to write with their right hands, something that seems downright cruel today. We need a similar revolution to turn around the treatment of those with ADHD[93] so that medication is a decision made from a position of informed choice, not because it is unavailable to those too unsure to seek help in the first place for their "brain-based shame", as Solden describes it. Likewise if schools can overcome their attachment to hiving off "naughty" pupils to isolation, and work more closely with parents and child and adolescent mental health care to identify where ADHD might be part of a picture, then perhaps some 25% of the prison population who are estimated to have ADHD[94] may be supported to improve their educational prospects and their job choices early on, with the benefit of medication.

We all make our mark in different ways, and if 95% choose to work one way, that doesn't make the other 5% any less valid for contributing differently. Consider the *volte-face* made in the face of the coronavirus pandemic, when suddenly the whole of society in lockdown came out of their front doors weekly to clap the contribution of some of the lowest paid workers in society, on

---

93 Membership of ADHD Action is one place to start. https://www.adhdaction.org/

94 Young S, Cocallis KM. 'Attention Deficit Hyperactivity Disorder (ADHD) in the Prison System', *Curr Psychiatry Rep.* 21(6):41. (2019) doi:10.1007/s11920-019-1022-3

zero-hours contracts, who were suddenly the heroes in our midst. "NHS workers and key workers, you are incredible" said the posters, when barely two months before we would have considered their work equal to the minimum wage most received. The usual capitalist values of making money, climbing the corporate greasy pole, securing advantage over others were swept aside during the pandemic to celebrate compassion, bravery, and selflessness. I can guarantee that a number of those healthcare workers had ADHD, working in emergency rooms, intensive care or for longer hours than others, putting their energy and hyperfocus to good use.

Even if ADHD can be a bit annoying to the rest, disruptive or disturbing the peace, we need neurodiversity in this world to look at problems differently. It took the coronavirus for us all to look up to the skies and notice that we preferred our world smelling a little sweeter without pollution, or to see that we were capable of putting kindness towards the elderly and vulnerable before economic profit. We now know that we are capable of a great change of heart in a short space of time. So, irritants of the world unite, we have nothing to lose but our shame. And I may be late to the party, after a mid-life diagnosis, but I am grateful that I now have an understanding of some of the puzzles in my past. And can hopefully put that towards a more productive future. Better late than never.

TEN OF THE MOST COMMON MYTHS ABOUT ADHD

In 2019, ADDISS, the UK information service, gave October ADHD Awareness Month the slogan "ADHD is real". Because I know many of you may be reading this book backwards, particularly if you have ADHD, here are the ten most common myths about ADHD. For the extended version, head to the website: https://www.adhdisreal.org.

MYTH #1: ADHD DOESN'T EXIST

Dr Russell Barkley, clinical professor of psychiatry at the Virginia Treatment Centre, educator and practitioner has published twenty-three books on ADHD. He writes:

References to ADHD appear in medical textbooks going back to 1775, and there are more than 100,000 articles in science journals referencing it. The prefrontal lobe network, or executive brain, provides mental abilities necessary for goal-directed, future-oriented action, self-awareness, inhibition, working memory, emotional self-regulation, self-motivation, and planning/problem solving. As such, ADHD is linked to a nearly doubled risk of early mortality before the age of ten, and more than four times the risk of early deaths in adults before the age of forty-five.

MYTH #2: ADHD IS JUST AN EXCUSE FOR LAZINESS

Thomas E Brown, professor of psychiatry at the University of Southern California, is director of the Brown Clinic for ADHD and Related Disorders at Manhattan Beach, California. He writes:

ADHD often looks like a lack of willpower, an excuse for laziness, when it's not. ADHD is really a problem with the chemical dynamics of the brain, it's not under voluntary control. ADHD symptoms are the result of neural messages in the brain not being effectively transmitted unless the activity or task is something that is really interesting. If messages are not sufficient to activate a person, it is likely to make them seem unmotivated or lazy. For 80–90% of people with ADHD, medication can significantly improve such problems.

MYTH #3: ALL CHILDREN GROW OUT OF ADHD

Dr Russell Barkley writes:

Children diagnosed with ADHD are not likely to grow out of it. By adolescence around 80% are still highly symptomatic and impaired, and while some of the children may recover by the age of 21–27 or adulthood, around 50%–86% will still have the full disorder.

MYTH #4: CHILDREN WITH ADHD JUST NEED MORE DISCIPLINE

Professor Eric Taylor is emeritus professor of child and adolescent psychiatry at Kings College London and is recipient of the Heinrich Hoffman medal from the World ADHD Federation. He writes:

Improving discipline does not alter the core problems. Many trials have shown that behavioural interventions, such as learning to praise positive behaviour, encouragement to ignore minor misbehavior, providing consistent disciplinary consequences for major misbehaviour, does decrease disruptiveness, aggression, and disobedience. However, the same trials have also made it plain that improving discipline (not the same as punishment) does not alter the core problems of inattention and impulsiveness. ADHD itself continues, and with it, the long-term risks for social adjustment.

MYTH #5: RITALIN AND OTHER STIMULANT MEDICATIONS FOR ADHD LEAD TO ADDICTION

Professor Stephen Faraone is a professor in the department of psychiatry and neuroscience at the State University of New York, and president of the World Federation of ADHD. He writes:

About fifteen years ago, I reviewed all available studies and found no evidence that the use of stimulant medications for ADHD in childhood led to addictive disorders in adolescence or adulthood. Instead we found some evidence that the stimulant medications for ADHD protected patients from subsequent substance use disorder. So, the data are clear and unequivocal. When used orally and therapeutically, the stimulant medications for ADHD do not cause addiction. Instead, because these medications control the symptoms of ADHD, they reduce the likelihood that a child with ADHD will, eventually, develop subsequent addictive disorders.

MYTH #6: EVERYONE HAS A LITTLE ADHD

The American organisation ADDA, the world's leading ADHD foundation for adults writes:

The symptoms of ADHD exist within a continuum of typical human behaviour. Most people lose their keys from time to time, they tune out in meetings, they're late to class, and they have trouble delaying gratification. But these are not the same as ADHD. With ADHD the reason is neurological in origin, it's not a choice, a fluke or a bad day. For people with ADHD these behaviours are disruptive, and they happen more often, with greater intensity, severity, and chronicity than for people without ADHD.

MYTH #7: ADHD IS OVERDIAGNOSED

Professor Eric Taylor writes:

Epidemiological research has found that prevalence does not vary much between countries, and the most authoritative reviews of studies puts its prevalence at about 7% of children internationally. The differences are based mainly on diagnostic criteria and measurement methods adopted. The conservative implication is that more than half of the affected children at any one time have never been identified as such.

MYTH #8: ADHD IS CAUSED BY BAD PARENTING

Professor Stephen Faraone writes:

Parents do not cause ADHD. The disorder comes from the accumulation of many environmental and genetic risk factors – i.e. the genes we inherit from our parents and adverse environments to which we are exposed. The environmental risk factors for ADHD have been proved because identical twin studies show that the risk to the co-twin is not 100%. Scientists have discovered that many of the environmental risk factors occur very early in the development of the brain, for example children who have a complicated birth are at a higher risk for ADHD, especially if the complication affects the flow of oxygen to the brain. When children are exposed to toxins, e.g. lead, pesticide, pollution, that can also increase the risk for ADHD.

MYTH #9: ONLY BOYS HAVE ADHD

Clinical psychologist Dr Michelle Frank specialises in providing diagnostic and treatment services to individuals with ADHD and writes about how diagnosis figures are still lower for girls, although it affects both genders equally. She writes:

One reason is that girls are less likely to present with hyperactive behaviour compared to boys, and are more likely to be diagnosed with predominantly inattentive symptoms that can be overlooked or misperceived, for example in a classroom, where they are less likely to cause a disturbance. Women and girls with ADHD have a higher incidence of depression and anxiety, which could be to do with women exhibiting "internalizing behaviours", and are initially referred for treatment due to these symptoms, and ADHD may be missed.
A number of complex factors further influence the female experience of ADHD, such as fluctuating hormone levels, oestrogen in particular, which complicate how symptoms are seen.

MYTH #10: PEOPLE WITH ADHD JUST CAN'T CONCENTRATE

ADHD Coaches Organization INC writes:

People with ADHD can concentrate when they are interested in what they are doing. New, unusual or exciting things capture their interest, particularly when they are challenging, rewarding, and fast-moving. The problem is not a lack of attention, but difficulty sustaining attention – particularly when the task is boring. It is also common for individuals with ADHD to talk about intense moments of concentration called Hyperfocus. While in Hyperfocus, people may become oblivious to everything around them, including time, chores, or the surrounding environment.

APPENDIX

These diary entries were written after the nursery teacher had told me she thought Michael, aged four, had ADHD, and I had decided to spend a week giving him some special attention to prove to myself he was absolutely fine.

WEDNESDAY 13 APRIL, 2005 (DAY THREE OF GOLDEN TIME)

Changing a family pattern is a very hard thing to do, but because today I am behaving as a born-again mother, fighting off any whiff of ADHD in Mikey, after the nursery teacher suggested it, and keeping the health visitor at bay, I am determined to do it. No way, I said to Miss K, give me a week to work on it, I'll show you that he hasn't got it. So now, I am on it. It is day three of my new regime of spending an hour's Golden Time in the morning with Michael before nursery, and I am refusing to let the cracks show. Especially as today he has waved the possibility under my nose that he does definitely have "impulsive" urges.

Take the full glass of water he took off the table at breakfast this morning, and promptly emptied on the floor. Unprovoked, but with an audience of H [Michael's elder brother], he timed the spill in the middle of the school rush hour, and left me skidding towards the lunchboxes with a hangover (the previous night I'd crashed out in the bath again, waking to chilly water at 1 am). Not my most controlled moment, but I refused to allow this to derail my new determination.

My friend Lois noticed this urge that he gets – the urge to create chaos where once there was order – when he tipped paint on the carpet at her house. 'He doesn't mean it,' said Lois (generously, bless her), 'it's just like there's a little switch in his head that goes off, and then he can't stop himself.'

Then, after I'd cleaned his impulsive breakfast spill, padding about in newly dampened socks, I bravely tried to continue in my born-again-Mother-Mild mode and got down the chocolate brownie mix to make cakes for the nursery cake sale. The recipe (if you could call it that) required five tablespoons of water. I filled a pint bottle, ready to measure "numbers" with Michael as part of our Golden Time Togetherness, and, as I turned to appease [his twin] Millie that she will get her turn at another point ... he pours the whole pint into the mixture.

Pushing him off the chair in my efforts to save the gooey chocolatey mass, I whisk the bowl from under his nose – and he cries as he hits the floor. I didn't get cross, because I am not that type of mother (at the moment), and, regardless, I did rather reluctantly continue with the original mission and stick the runny version of the recipe into the oven.

Before I had time to consider whether two incidents in Golden Time amount to some malign impulsivity that was part of the Hyperactivity Disorder, Mikey stuck his hand in the empty bowl of mixture and turned to wipe his fingers on my white dressing gown.

Three strikes, and he was out. Determined not to lose my temper again, I told him that "baking with Mummy" was over, and could he please piss off and watch telly now.

THURSDAY 14 APRIL, 2005 (DAY FOUR OF GOLDEN TIME)

Golden Time today finds me stressed out, attempting to dress the children, give them breakfast, and tidy the kitchen before the arrival of the au pair at 9am. I need the head start to carve out that Golden Time half-hour with Michael. While Millie goes off to buy hairclips from the chemist with the au pair, I snip madly away at pieces of paper with the name of Michael and six of his classmates so he can learn to recognise them. I place the names down on the table and turn them over – like a memory game. The clock is ticking; if I can keep his attention for twenty minutes, surely that promises something, right? An example of how he hasn't got Attention Deficit, perhaps? We hit the twenty minutes. Michael is still playing, and can now recognise not only his own name, but also that of two other twins in the nursery – Poppy and Arthur. Phew. At last he can find his name and stick it on the Velcro wall as he comes into nursery – a government early-learning target, apparently. I am feeling momentarily less panicked. I have taught him more in twenty minutes than the teachers have managed in two terms.

FRIDAY 15 APRIL, 2005 (DAY FIVE OF GOLDEN TIME)

By the end of the week, doing other, similarly jolly activities – painting ('Can I do my rainbow in all black, Mummy?') and numbers on a wooden clock ('Is the number 'A', Mummy?') – the Golden Time is turning into a leaden one. I'm feeling completely nonplussed by this so-called behavioural disorder, and look instead to the teacher to see what her problem must be.

Meanwhile, me attending to Michael's delivery to school to show off his proficiency of sticking his name to his coat rack instead of his schoolfriends has got me two parking tickets. However, not all is lost: speaking to the other mothers, instead of avoiding them, has made me see that there are quite a few complaints about the nursery teacher Miss K.

'Yes, a couple of the mothers thought about going along to the head and complaining about her', said one – a comment that felt like pouring soothing honey on my troubled soul. Whatever their problems with her were, she certainly couldn't cope with naughty four-year-old boys and was quick to push the problem back on the parents – or, worse, the child, I reflected.

After a week of this Golden Time business, I felt quite cross that our society brands children who are deemed round pegs incapable of fitting into its square holes – by the age of only four! Whatever happened to "character"? I railed inwardly. Wasn't this something to be encouraged, not crushed? I put on my best power jacket with shoulder pads and went in to see the teacher. 'I have spent a whole week with Michael, giving him stars for effort and spending one-on-one time with him, and I can report that there is nothing wrong with him. He just needs attention.'

'But as you can see,' she countered, 'I have twenty other children to look after, so I can't necessarily give him that attention.' I'd said my piece, and I turned on my heels to leave. It had been a panic-stricken week from hell, with not a shred of work to my name, and I just wanted it over. Perhaps it is time for another school move.

As you can see from these extracts, denial is a powerful thing. I was terrified of the stigma and labelling of Michael, but I didn't realise that going forward there would be a lot of positives to having his diagnosis. With it, the class teacher would have had to have differentiated for him and given him that special attention. Now as a secondary school teacher, I am aware of the benefits, but I wasn't ready to hear about them back then, and everyone has to go through their own process to find their way through this complex condition.

RECOMMENDED READING

I have chosen the following books because they are all "strengths-based", or tackle the subject of ADHD with humour. These are the only type I find helpful.

***Women with Attention Deficit Disorder* by Sari Solden (Underwood Books)**
Updated in 2005, this 1995 classic was the first book that lifted the lid on the lives of many women who had suffered in silence. It is extraordinary to read because it often feels as if it is describing your own internal monologue, or painting a picture of your personal never-before-discussed dramas. The follow-up *A Radical Guide for Women with ADHD* is a great self-help workbook without a hint of blame or finger-pointing.

***Queen of Distraction: How Women with ADHD Can Conquer Chaos, Find Focus and Get More Done* by Terry Matlen (New Harbinger Publications)**
Psychotherapist and ADHD life coach Matlen tackles issues like shopping, cooking, managing clutter, and the minutiae of everyday life with a forensic energy. I normally rebel against any bossy suggestions for order, but her tone and knowledge about ADHD wins me over every time.

***All Dogs have ADHD* by Kathy Hoopmann (Jessica Kingsley Publishers)**
I love this book, although it is all captions and photos of dogs. I just wish they had added some real bitches in there, so not every

caption began with "He". Once you see the connection between ADHD and dogs, however, you can't help but notice it in every park you visit.

***The Couple's Guide to Thriving with ADHD* by Melissa Orlov and Nancie Kohlenberger (Specialty Press, Inc.)**
This is a follow-up to Orlov's *The ADHD Effect on Marriage*, and is packed with interesting insights behind the net curtain of an ADHD relationship. It has a particularly good chapter on anger and ADHD, a cause of many divorces.

***The Gift of Adult ADHD: How to Transform Your Challenges and Build on Your Strengths* by Lara Honos-Webb (New Harbinger Publications)**
Relentlessly positive, this is the only book I've found that tackles some of the more away-with-the-fairies aspects of ADHD, such as "interpersonal intuition" and "visions" that guide some ADHDers in their certainty over decision-making, plus the "gift of ecological consciousness". It does a great job of reframing the three traits of distractibility, restlessness, and impulsivity as creativity, exuberance, and emotional sensitivity.

***Movers, Dreamers and Risk-Takers: Unlocking the Power of ADHD* by Kevin Roberts (Hazelden Publishing)**
"Those with ADHD have a predisposition to confronting the challenges of life and a deep preference for perceiving the world creatively" – this is Roberts' take, and combined with his sense of humour makes him one of my favourite speakers on the subject. In my mind, he is the poster boy for ADHD, and his other book *Cyber Junkie: Escape the Gaming and Internet Trap* is a must read for anyone who has experienced the darker downside of hyperfocus.

Driven to Distraction: Recognizing and Coping with Attention Deficit Disorder from Childhood through

***Adulthood* by Dr Edward Hallowell and John Ratey (Anchor Books)**
Updated in 2011, both psychiatrists have ADHD and have written the most reassuring and comprehensive guide to the disorder, deserving of its *New York Times* bestseller status, without descending into doom and gloom.

***ADHD: What Everyone Needs to Know* by Stephen Hinshaw and Katherine Ellison (Oxford University Press)**
In intelligent and accessible prose, the Pulitzer-prize-winning journalist Ellison and the expert Professor Hinshaw ask all the questions that might nag you, such as what are the side-effects of stimulants, and what is the ADHD Industrial Complex (the unregulated market place where snake oils are offered as a fix for the disorder)? It is a one-stop shop for people who suspect that they may have ADHD.

***The Tipping Points: What Professionals Should Recognize as the Social Impact of ADHD* by Phil Anderton (ADDISS)**
Phil Anderton has come to the subject after serving twenty-seven years in the UK police service, and manages to take a combined approach of great practicality and immense compassion for the sufferers. He highlights some often-overlooked aspects of ADHD such as driving safety, problematic drug use, and crime.

***The ADHD Advantage: What You Thought Was a Diagnosis May Be Your Greatest Strength* by Dale Archer, MD (Avery Publishing)**
Psychiatrist and ADHDer Dale Archer champions the "curious, resilient, visionary" nature of the condition – and how it has bred a number of successful entrepreneurs. Archer refuses to treat his own ADHD with medication, so is wedded to the idea of putting the energy to good use.

MEMOIRS

Buzz: A Year of Paying Attention **by Katherine Ellison (Hyperion Books)**

This memoir by Ellison tries umpteen different goods and services sold by the modern mental health industry to help herself and her son, aged twelve, with their ADHD. Few work, but there is plenty of humour and insight along the way.

Hiding an Elephant: Living with Adult ADHD **by Kim A Gay (Tate Publishing)**

To be consumed in one sitting, this is an honest account of the disorganisation and overwhelm that many women and mothers can suffer as they tend to a family, and how it drove one woman to isolate herself from others until she became depressed and suicidal. She overcomes these feelings of shame to offer up her story as an example of transformation.

Sane New World: Taming the Mind **by Ruby Wax (Hodder & Stoughton)**

Ruby Wax is a comic genius and recently retrained in neuroscience, resulting in this book about taming the mind, and particularly about mindfulness training. "The brain is like a pliable piece of playdough; you can resculpt it by breaking old mental habits and creating new, more flexible ways of thinking", she writes. And her research on neuroplasticity is fascinating.

Beneath the Surface: My Story **by Michael Phelps (Sports Publishing)**

Michael Phelps is an Olympic legend, and his story is worth reading because he has overcome so much, and trained so hard, to be decorated with so many medals. An inspiration to all ADHDers everywhere.

ACKNOWLEDGEMENTS

I am indebted to my family Adam, Millie, Michael, and Humphrey, and my mother Josephine Mahony and twin brother Dominic Mahony MBE. I also have to thank profusely readers of earlier drafts of the book: my father John Mahony, and daughter Millie Barker, authors Susan Johnson and Paul Richardson, as well as dear friends Catherine Lees and Katy Emck OBE. The play of the book, *Late to the Party*, which preceded publication also shaped this final version, and was a team effort, so thanks to all those who helped to stage it: director Hendrick January, actors Kelvin O'Mard and Michael Bramley, friends Sarah Homer, Belinda Chapman, Sally Mayhew, as well as the late great Tessa Tennant OBE, who gave us rehearsal space and put us up during the Edinburgh Fringe performance. Other cheerleaders who helped make this book happen include writing coach Rami Vance, Maria Coyle, Sham Sandhu, Clive Goodyear and Rachel Kelly, as well as contributors Joyce Blake, Clarissa Vorfeld, Dr Ari Tuckman, Andrea Bilbow OBE, Dr James Arkell, Rory Bremner, Dr Stephen Hinshaw, and Dr Judith Mohring. Finally, a big thanks to my agent Jason Bartholomew, editor Dawn Bates, and publisher Jo Lal, and all those at Trigger especially Beth James, Rachel Gregory and Lyndsey Mayhew. Your belief in this mental health issue matters.